THE UNTOLD STORY
of Palestinian Christians

S0-AEQ-366

JACK KINCAID with Ron Brackin

Unless noted otherwise, Scripture quotations in this publication
are from the Holy Bible, New International Version®, Copyright ©
1973, 1978, 1984 International Bible Society. Used by permission
of Zondervan Bible Publishers.

All rights reserved. No part of this publication may be repro-
duced, stored in a retrieval system or transmitted in any form or
by any means without the prior permission of the publisher.

Copyright © 2002 by Jack Kincaid
Banner Communications, Inc.
9417 NW 43rd Street, Suite D-4
Gainesville, FL   32653

ISBN 0-9725258-0-7

Printed in the United States of America

To the Palestinian believers who made this book possible and to suffering and persecuted believers worldwide – "whom God is not ashamed to be called their God." (Hebrews 11:16)

Contents

Introduction

A word is worth a thousand pictures.

Say the word "Bogart" to anyone over 50 and you conjure images of Rick's American Café in exotic Casablanca; or a Canadian adventurer pulling a wannabe wooden warship through steamy, slug-infested shallows. You see steel-helmeted, Camel-smoking GIs, no-nonsense gangsters, pragmatic private investigators and a jewel-encrusted falcon hidden under a coat of black enamel.

Say the word "Holocaust," and boxcars roll into view, packed with parents and children, businessmen, barbers, artists and musicians. Electrified gates secure concentration camps bristling with razor wire. Helmeted guards pace and push and shout. Iron oven doors swing open to reveal charred human bones. Tiled shower rooms facilitate ethnic cleansing. Striped uniforms hang from breathing skeletons. Mind numbing mass graves swallow families and villages. Mountains of gold fillings and wedding rings glitter. And empty eyes stare through fences at Allied cameras.

The power and depth of a single word. But not all words conjure accurate pictures.

Say the word "Palestinian," for example, and you will probably envision Yasser Arafat in olive-green, glaring out from under a black and white checkered kaffiyeh. Boys throwing stones at tanks and soldiers. Flaming flags and effigies. Bloody hands proudly exhibited from a second story window. Snipers and suicide bombers.

But these images depict only a tiny segment of the millions of people who call themselves Palestinians.

Say "evangelical Palestinian Christian," and you may get no image at all. Trying to discuss evangelical Palestinian Christians with a Westerner is like trying to talk to a Nubian about snowmen.

Neither has ever heard of one, never seen one, and really can't imagine what one might be like.

It is difficult, if not impossible, for an American Christian to visualize a Palestinian Arab on his knees, praising the name of Jesus; or a Palestinian Arab reading the Bible to her children. Or Palestinian churches with altars and worship music and sermons, childcare, Sunday school and fellowship meals. And he would undoubtedly be surprised to meet a Palestinian Arab alumnus of Fuller Theological Seminary in Pasadena.

The pages that follow, therefore, are filled with word-pictures, a week's worth of snapshots of evangelical Palestinian Christians – born-again men and women who love Jesus Christ and live among Muslims and traditional Christians in the West Bank and Gaza Strip. Believers who pay dearly for their faith.

These are disciples of Jesus in whose hearts echo the words of Paul to the saints in Rome: "I could wish that I myself were cursed and cut off from Christ for the sake of my brothers, those of my own race . . ." (Romans 9:3).

While Paul saw the terms as synonymous, today in the Middle East it is necessary to distinguish between "brothers" and "those of my own race" – that is, between "believers" and "Christians."

Charles M. Sennott, former Middle East bureau chief for *The Boston Globe* and author of *The Body and the Blood*, was intrigued that "it was so common to hear adamant Palestinian secularists and atheists refer to themselves as Christians. The same was true, of course, of secular Jews and Muslims in Israel, who referred to themselves by the faiths into which they were born, even though they themselves did not necessarily adhere to or even believe in that faith. In this sense, religion here is a cultural point of reference—more a statement of where one comes from than a set of beliefs that define who one is."

Rabbi David Forman, co-founder of Rabbis for Human Rights, summed it up in an interview with Sennott. "Religion," he said, "has become nationalized in this land." [1]

Few books examine the Palestinian side of the Middle East

conflict. Fewer still consider the perspective of traditional Arab Christians in the historical churches of Palestine. And to my knowledge, no author has ever walked a mile in the shoes of evangelical Palestinian Christians – the minority of minorities.

To correct this omission, *Between Two Fires*© provides a forum for these brothers and sisters to tell their story in their own words and share with us in the West the commission God has set before them.

The focus of the book will be Palestinian, unabashedly one-sided. It will not attempt to balance the Palestinian perspective with the view from the Israeli side, since thousands of books, countless motion pictures and a growing number of heartbreaking memorials powerfully and thoroughly depict the history, theology, culture, viewpoint and suffering of the Jewish people.

Frankly, I had hoped even to completely avoid the political and nationalistic issues. But they are inseparable from the woof and warp of the Middle East fabric and will prove useful for Western Christians to understand the motives, struggles and hearts of our Palestinian brethren.

In the absence of journalistic parity, then, the reader might be tempted to take sides. If so, remember that neither the Israelis nor the Palestinians are always right. Both have inexcusably violated – and continue to violate – the laws of God and man. The Lord has called us to love and understand them, not to judge between them.

Besides, for the evangelical believer, there is only one side:

> "Now when Joshua was near Jericho, he looked up and saw a man standing in front of him with a drawn sword in his hand. Joshua went up to him and asked, 'Are you for us or for our enemies?' 'Neither,' he replied, 'but as commander of the army of the Lord I have now come.'" (Joshua 5:13-14).

Today, Jericho is part of the West Bank, and both Israelis and Palestinians still ask of God: "Are you for us or for our enemies?"

Not surprisingly, God's answer is the same today as it was 14 centuries before Christ. As one preacher paraphrased it: "I have not come to take *sides*; I have come to take *over*."

God is on neither side. His plan is to bring both Israelis and Palestinians – Jew, Muslim, tribal Christian and atheist – over to His side.

It is important to remember that living in the Holy Land does not make one holy any more than living in the desert makes one a camel. Most of those living in Israel and in Palestine are secular and in desperate need of salvation.

God has, however, preserved a remnant. Jewish believers are his instruments in Israel, as Arab believers are in Palestine. Both are members of God's family, our brothers and sisters. And both are entitled to our understanding, acceptance, love, prayers and support.

If you are a lover of Israel, by all means continue to love Israel. Your Palestinian brethren encourage you to do so. They ask only that you spread your arms just a little wider to embrace them as well.

Notes

[1] Charles M. Sennott, *The Body and the Blood* (Public Affairs, New York, 2001), pp. 152-153, 425.

May 7

And if a stranger sojourn with thee in your land, ye shall not do him wrong. The stranger that sojourneth with you shall be unto you as the home-born among you, and thou shalt love him as thyself; for ye were strangers in the land of Egypt: I am the LORD your God. *The Torah* (Leviticus 19:33-34)

Ron Brackin and I boarded the Continental jetliner in Newark at 10:50 last night. There was plenty of room to stretch out and sleep since few tourists visit Israel these days. Most of our traveling companions were Jews or Arabs on their way home.

I, too, felt that I was returning home. Over the past five years, I had been to the Holy Land many times, fulfilling a dream that began before Israel even existed.

My mother is a wonderful godly woman who knows her Bible and made sure her family does too. One thing she taught us was to love Jewish people.

"God said He would bless those who bless Israel," she reminded us again and again. "So you must always be kind to Jews." Understandably, I grew up longing to visit Israel.

Most of my professional life was spent in broadcasting. I worked for CBN in Boston for a few years, then left to launch an independent television station in West Virginia. We used much of our profits to establish media ministries, provide humanitarian aid and build churches around the world.

One year, while visiting Canadian broadcaster David Maines, I was introduced to his son-in-law, an evangelical Palestinian Christian named Nizar Shaheen (Ni-zahr' Shah-heen'). Nizar is a strong spiritual leader and Bible scholar who hails originally from Cana, Scripture's water-to-wine city in Galilee.

Nizar and I hit it off from day one. We talked, we called each other, we wrote. He shared with me his passion to make the gospel available to the 3.3 million Palestinians in the West Bank and Gaza Strip and ultimately to all of the Arab-speaking people of the Middle East. And it wasn't long before Nizar's passion became mine.

He moved his family back to Galilee, and I sold the television station and formed a 501(c)(3) ministry called Banner Communications, Inc.

Shortly after that, my lifelong dream came true as I boarded a plane for my first trip to Israel.

There in Galilee, Nizar and I launched a television program called *Light of Life,* currently broadcast on the SAT-7, Arab-language satellite network and the Sudanese National Television Network.

To date, we have produced on location two 52-part series – one on the life of Christ; the other on John's Gospel. Both are in Arabic and also have been packaged into a VHS discipleship packet with accompanying study guides for distribution to Arab-language churches throughout Israel and the Middle East. The Sermon on the Mount and other stories from the New Testament are in the works.

A year into the project, we launched International Media Services (IMS), a Jerusalem-based production company that enables us to avoid the high costs of renting equipment and facilities. A talented and dedicated Swede named Len Johansson came on board as CEO. So while I ping-pong between Israel and the States devoting most of my time to Banner Communications, Len and Nizar run things overseas.

During one visit, I joined an intercessory tour led by a Messianic Jew named Reuven Doren, author of the best-selling book, *One New Man*.

In Samaria (West Bank), we approached a high hill or *tel* where we were to spend time in prayer and intercession. A fine new road led up to a beautiful Jewish settlement, complete with its own grocery store, schools and community swimming pool.

The road passed through a small Palestinian village – really little more than ten shacks with outdoor plumbing and, in some cases, outdoor cooking. I had never seen such wretched poverty. I learned that the land had been taken away from these families by the Israeli government to build the settlement, the road into it and a security zone around it.

I saw and heard things I did not want to see and hear. And when I did, I was afraid to give them honest consideration because they threatened my long-held beliefs and opinions.

In the weeks after the tour, I found myself listening more attentively when evangelical Palestinian Christians reproved me for closing my ears to them.

"We're not the enemy," they said. "We're your brothers. We're hurting, and you won't listen because you're so blinded by your end-time theology."

They were right. My eschatology was whitewashing the injustices that were all around me. I also became aware that I subtly had begun to take responsibility for Israel's destiny, instead of trusting God to work things out His way, in His time.

I didn't want to see Israel as a secular state – or Palestinians as people. I was more comfortable picturing Jesus walking Israel's streets and fields and visualizing all Palestinians as terrorists. I desperately wanted all Jews to wear white kippahs and all Arabs to wear black kaffiyehs. I needed everything to be clear and simple. I wanted it to be easy to choose sides.

But the regional issues are far too complex for that. Besides, I had already chosen sides when I became a Christian. I chose God's side. God loves Jews *and* Arabs, including the terrorists on both sides – the Irgun and Stern Gang, Hamas, Tanzim and Islamic Jihad. And my choice required that I pray for and support my brothers and sisters in Israel *and* in Palestine.

Most of us in the West, however, have no idea that there *are* evangelical Christian believers in the West Bank and Gaza Strip who love Jesus Christ with all their hearts and sacrifice everything they have for His sake.

*   *   *   *

That's when I felt God leading me to write a book. But I needed help, and the Lord sent Ron Brackin.

Ron's credentials include Washington broadcast journalist, congressional press secretary, a decade of fundraising for major international Christian ministries, work with the persecuted church worldwide, a pile of articles and several books. Most important, he has a passion for the work God is doing in the Middle East.

It took only one phone call. He was interested and available.

We arrived at 4:15 p.m. on May 7 at Ben Gurion International Airport in Tel Aviv, rented a car, and drove up Rte.1 to Jerusalem. It was Ron's first time in Israel, and he was one big eye and ear. He had been in the Middle East only once before but like Moses, had gotten no closer to Israel than Mount Nebo in what is today Amman, Jordan. The first thing he learned is that one always travels *up* to Jerusalem, whether north, south, east or west of the city.

To me, every visit is like returning to an old and cherished friend. At the same time, it's like meeting someone I've wanted to meet all my life.

In May, Israel is still green and lush, before the sun toasts the grass like coconut. The big green road signs read like a Bibleland glossary in Hebrew, Arabic and English. I wanted to stop and show Ron the sites, but we had very little time and a lot to do. He would have to come as a tourist another, and hopefully safer, time.

Despite rush hour traffic, we were in sight of the City of Gold within an hour. By statute, all the buildings in Jerusalem are required to be made of Jerusalem stone, a unique native rock that gives off a warm aura in the afternoon sun and makes the city appear to have been caressed by King Midas.

We pulled up in front of the Hyatt Regency on Lehi Street, a block from IMS offices on the *green line* and checked in. The "green" or "truce" line marks the divisions of historic Palestine after the 1948 war. It has been repositioned several times and appears on today's tourist maps as a trail of dashes separating Israel from the West Bank and Gaza Strip and dividing Jerusalem into Jewish West and Arab East.

On the front wall outside the hotel entrance hung several tour banners, but they were mostly for show. There were virtually no tourists in Israel now, and the hotel was all but empty. Its reputation once focused on its accommodations; now it is known as the hotel where Israeli Tourism Minister Rehavam Ze'evi was assassinated. Four men accused of the killing and tried in Ramallah remain in Palestinian custody, overseen by British and American observers, while Israel argues for their extradition.

Ron and I settled into our rooms before meeting Len Johansson for dinner.

Pashas is a typical Arab restaurant in East Jerusalem. Despite the poverty of the Palestinian half of the city, the restaurants are second to none, as is their classic Arab fare – from the array of to-die-for breads, falafel and a dozen other spreads, to the lamb, chicken and shish-kebob, finished off with thick, sweet Arab coffee, ripe watermelon, and, for those so inclined, an apple-scented *nargila* or water pipe.

The division between East and West Jerusalem is a snapshot of what has come to be known over the past half century as the Middle East Crisis. Two sides of the city, two sides of the story, two distinct peoples with the same roots.

The area known by some as "Palestine" and referred to by others as "the occupied territories" is made up of two isolated areas that have undergone several iterations since the United Nations and Great Britain carved out an independent state for Israel in 1947.

The Gaza Strip is a tiny piece of real estate on the shores of the Mediterranean, its southern tip bordering on Egypt. The West Bank — biblical Judea and Samaria — lies in central-eastern Israel and runs roughly from the southern tip of the Dead Sea to a point about halfway between Haifa and Tel-Aviv.

At dinner, we discussed the current situation, known as the Al-Aksa Intifada, and some of the history leading up to it.

Intifada is an Arabic word meaning *uprising* or *a shaking off*. This is the second such uprising since the 1967 Six-Day War. The first intifada began in 1987 and continued until 1992.

The spark that touched off the latest intifada was ignited on the morning of September 28, 2000, when Israeli Prime Minister Ariel Sharon, protected by a cordon of security guards and a thousand Israeli border police and special forces, crossed the plaza of the Western Wall and began to ascend the ramp to the Temple Mount.

This site is particularly sacred to both Jews and Muslims. To the former, it is *Har Habayit*, the Temple Mount; to the latter, it is *Haram esh-Sharif*, the Noble Sanctuary. Both religions believe it to be the biblical Mount Moriah upon which Abraham was prepared to offer to God his son, Isaac. Jews, however, revere it as the probable site of the Holy of Holies of the Second Temple, while Muslims honor it as *masjid al-aksa*, the "furthermost sanctuary," from which the Prophet Muhammad ascended to heaven.

Prime Minister Sharon is also symbolic for both sides. To the Jews, he is a war hero, wounded in the 1948 Arab-Israeli War, liberator of Jerusalem in the Six-Day War and general of Israeli Defense Forces in Lebanon. He is also revered as the engineer of a circle of Jewish settlements surrounding the Holy City.

His "strategy" was to first plunk down trailer homes, then move in soldiers to protect the first pioneers, and then develop self-standing communities where only Israeli citizens lived. These would be surrounded by more military barricades, which would require the seizure of additional land.

"The Israeli policy of supporting the construction of new Jewish settlements in the occupied West Bank and Gaza was not born simply out of a need for more housing for Jews. There was plenty of open land to the west of Jerusalem, and vast reserves in the Negev and the Galilee that Israel was not bothering to develop. This was a policy designed to establish an Israeli foothold on what the settlement movement saw as land God promised to Jews. It was a policy carried out in the belief that once Jews were living there, it would be difficult, perhaps impossible, to make them move." [1]

Sharon is symbolic to Palestinians as well, albeit a symbol of injustice and oppression. And his presence at Islam's third holiest site was viewed by religious Muslims as a desecration.

As Sharon ascended to the Mount, a hail of rocks beat down from hundreds of *shebab*, or Palestinian youths, on the platform above. The Israelis responded with tear gas and "rubber bullets" – steel pellets coated with hard plastic.

Fortunately, no one was killed that day. But death and mourning were not far behind.

It was not long before Palestinian suicide bombers began to terrorize Israeli civilians on the streets, in restaurants and riding public transportation; Israeli Defense Forces (IDF) retaliating with retributive incursions into Palestine that terrorized Arab neighborhoods.

The roots of the Al-Aqsa Intifada, however, extend much deeper than September, 2000.

Some observers dig as far as Genesis 17:8, long before the Roman conquest, when the land was occupied by "the Canaanites, Hittites, Amorites, Perizzites, Hivites and Jebusites" – when God gave Abraham and his descendants "the whole land of Canaan" as "an everlasting possession."

It was not called Palestine then. In fact, this term does not appear until A.D. 105 [2] when Emperor Trajan dubbed the region between the Mediterranean Sea and the Jordan River *Palaestina Tertia*, the Land of Palestine, a name derived from the Philistines who lived along the southern seacoast.

Throughout the centuries, many flags and banners have flown over the region.

After deliverance from slavery in Egypt, the Hebrews conquered the land. Then in 930 B.C., the Jewish kingdom split into Israel and Judah, with ten tribes in the north and two in the south. Assyria whittled away at Israel from 721 B.C. to 715 B.C., and Judah was taken into captivity by Babylon in 587 B.C..

A half-century later, Persia conquered the Babylonians and sent the Jews back to Jerusalem. In 332 B.C., Alexander the Great took over until the Jewish revolt of 167 B.C.. In 63 B.C., Rome conquered Jerusalem.

Constantine Christianized the region in the fourth century A.D.

After another two centuries, Islam was born, and within 20 years of the Prophet Mohammed's death in 632, the new religion had seized power.

In 1099, Jerusalem fell to the European Crusaders, only to be recaptured by the Muslims in 1187. The Ottoman Turks took not only Palestine but Syria and Egypt as well in 1516.

The first Zionists arrived from Eastern Europe in 1882.

The Turks, who had aligned themselves with Germany during World War I, were displaced by Great Britain. And in 1917, the British issued the Balfour Declaration, promising the Jews a national homeland in Palestine and mandating respect for the civil and religious rights of non-Jews, some of whose families had lived there for millennia.

In November 1947, the United Nations voted to partition Palestine, "now occupied by about 1 million Muslims, 600,000 Jews and 150,000 Christians." It was divided into Jewish and Arab areas, with Jerusalem declared to be international territory. [3]

Six months later, the British Mandate over Palestine ended. Israel became an autonomous state (Appendix III), and war broke out with the Arabs.

In short, the history of Palestine is somebody taking the land from somebody else only to lose it to somebody else and somebody else again. It is a history that has been written many different – even conflicting – ways. At the same time, it is a history that is passed on from generation to generation of those who live there, with bitterness and a burning quest for justice.

Nothing fully compares to the history of Palestine.

In some ways, it resembles the history of pioneer America. Native Americans, too, lost the land on which they had lived for generations. They, too, were both victims and perpetrators of atrocities. Their descendants, too, live on reservations chiseled out for them.

In other ways, Palestine's history is like that of apartheid South Africa.

Comparisons, however, are always inadequate, historical reconstructions incomplete and political analyses unproductive.

As we ate our watermelon, we returned to the bottom line. We were here not to take sides or point fingers. We were here to learn about God's people and His unique plan for them.

Notes

[1] Charles M. Sennott, *The Body and the Blood* (Public Affairs, New York, 2001), pp. 121-122.

[2] Bernard Lewis, *The Arabs in History* (Harper Torchbooks, Harper & Row, Publishers, New York, 1966), p. 26.

[3] Most of the preceding historical chronology was taken from Jimmy Carter, *The Blood of Abraham* (The University of Arkansas Press, 1993), p. xiv.

May 8

If anyone says, "I love God," yet hates his brother, he is a liar. 1 John 4:20

ITEM: Fifteen people were killed last night in a suicide bombing at the Cafeteria Snooker Club in Rishon Lezion's New Industrial Zone, just south of Tel Aviv. At least 40 others were wounded. Hamas claimed responsibility.

That's as far as the world news services took these events. But here in Israel, the victims are not just statistics. They're people like you and I. Their friends and family members know them — and mourn them — by name: Avi Bayaz, Shoshana Magmari, Dahlia Masa, Haim Rafael. Yisrael Shikar. Anat Trempatush. Rasan Sharouk.

The Jerusalem Post reminded us of the humanity — and inhumanity — of this intifada: "Still in shock, Eliahu Shikri searched for his wife, Pnina, in a Rishon Lezion pool hall until he found her in the dark among the dead bodies. Knowing she was dead, he still held her, caressing and hugging her until the doctor came."

ITEM: Today is Jerusalem Day, marking 36 years since the reunification of Jerusalem. The festivities begin tonight at sundown. Only Israelis have reason to celebrate.

ITEM: The standoff at the fourth-century Church of the Nativity in Bethlehem is in its thirty-sixth day. Yesterday, Italy briefly reneged on its promise to accept thirteen Palestinians slated for deportation, and today the on-again/off-again settlement is on again. IDF soldiers have already dismantled the huge surveillance crane erected in Manger Square to monitor inside the church and have removed the metal detectors from their positions near the "Door of Humility."

"We are in touch with the people," says Labib Madanat, General Secretary of the Palestinian Bible Society. "We are faced every day with the bitter situation. But we refuse to succumb to despair. Jesus is our living hope. And through His Word, we want to serve this hope to the Palestinian people."

Ron and I met for breakfast with our host and guide Labib Madanat (Lah-beeb' Mah-da-naht'), General Secretary of the Palestinian Bible Society.   Tomorrow we will try to enter Bethlehem. Today, we are going into Ramallah.

*   *   *   *

Crowds cheered last Thursday as Palestinian Chairman Yasser Arafat finally emerged from his shattered compound.

Today, as we entered the city, no one was cheering. People were still cleaning up the debris left behind after a month of IDF occupation, which began March 29. This retaliatory incursion was touched off by a Hamas terrorist attack that murdered 21 people and wounded more than 170 at a Passover dinner Wednesday night in Netanya. Four more people were slaughtered Thursday at the Alon Moreh Jewish settlement near Nablus.

Early Friday morning, Israel launched Operation Defensive Shield – the army's largest offensive since the war in Lebanon – unleashing four armored divisions into the West Bank. Fifty-ton Merkeva tanks and massive D-9 armored bulldozers thundered into the Palestinian capital of Ramallah and began demolishing fences and walls surrounding Arafat's compound.

By the end of the siege, *The Jerusalem Post* reported 29 IDF soldiers dead and 127 wounded. Dozens of Palestinians had been killed and 4,200 detained with 1,300 still in custody. Twenty-three bomb workshops and hundreds of explosive belts were discovered. Thousands of guns, machine guns, mortars, Kassam missiles and launchers, ammunition and other war materiel were said to have been confiscated.

Ramallah looked like a war zone. Homes, stores and multi-storied buildings were razed or gutted. Tank cannons and explosives had blown the city to pieces. Seven buildings around the government house were bombed. Huge piles of debris covered city blocks. Cars and trucks were crushed or tossed aside like Hot Wheel toys. Pavement was chewed up and spit out by heavy steel tank treads.

Ahmed Qureia, Palestinian Parliament speaker and one of the architects of the Oslo Accords (Appendix V), estimated the damage at more than $500 million. Other Palestinian officials said it was too early to evaluate the extent of the destruction.

*   *   *   *

About 40,000 people live in Ramallah, a seven-square-mile city built on several hills, ten miles north of Jerusalem.

Before the 1948 war, it was a Christian town. As a result of the war, thousands of Palestinian refugees came and settled. Now there are only two Evangelical churches left. One is near Ramallah Hospital.

When someone is shot, he is taken to this hospital. If he dies, the funeral leaves from the hospital, accompanied by high emotions, shooting and danger.

When Nader Ghneim (Nah'-der Gah-neem') was a boy, his family went to this church. Because of all the violence around the hospital, however, his family was afraid and stopped going, as did many others.

"I would go in sometimes," Nader recalls, "and there were only two or three people at the service, and they were the family of the pastor. Now, it is a little better."

Ramallah Local Church is one of only two evangelical churches in this once Christian city.

Today Nader and his family attend the other church – the Ramallah Local Church – where he serves as a youth worker. But decades of violence have taken their toll on the Christian population. Between October 2000 and November 2001 alone, 880 Christians emigrated from Ramallah. [1]

Now there is no one to play the organ, because the organist, like thousands of others, has fled to the United States or Canada, Europe or Australia. Most of the youth that were there ten years ago left with their families.

"In recent years," Nader says, "Muslims have been pouring into Ramallah, buying buildings and moving in. Only about 10,000 Christians of all denominations are left in the city. Very few are evangelical believers. In our church, only about 20 or 25 are believers out of more than 100 who attend.

"In 1992, during the Gulf War, 20 to 30 of our committed believers left. The church nearly died. Then it started growing until the current intifada. Now they are leaving again. We work with the remaining youth and encourage them to stay and try to live in the situation. Still, many families are leaving.

"Even my family, my mother and two sisters, went to Jerusalem to continue the process of immigration to the U.S. If you speak to any person here, they say they don't like to leave but at least they want to have an open door. It's too hard. With tanks around you, you can't go out of the house, and even your house is not safe.

"After one time when the soldiers came, a Christian visited me from Jerusalem, and I was just showing him around Ramallah, what they burned, what they bombed, what they did. At the end, I invited him to my house.

"When he came in, I said, 'Do you see that room? That's our safe room. It is well inside the house and protected. We stay in it.' But the other night, the Israeli soldiers were shooting outside, and a bullet entered our safe room. So you can see that our protection is gone. There really was never any protection. There is no safety."

Nader and his family fled the city this time when the tanks came into Ramallah.

"We were out of the house for 25 days. We ran to the mountains and were like refugees. Hundreds of people left Ramallah because they were very afraid. People were running in the streets after they heard that the Israelis were coming. It was really terrible. After we left, another curfew was imposed, forcing people to remain in their homes everyday for 23 hours of the 24 hours in each day. No one was able to go out.

"Even after we returned to Ramallah, it was two days before we could enter our house because it is very near Arafat's headquarters. We lived in my aunt's house until the debris could be cleared and we could move back in. It is a very bad situation. You cannot even sleep at night, because the Israeli soldiers keep shooting, just shooting for no reason throughout the night. Even inside my house, I could see the flashing of the guns and bombs as I lay awake."

In addition to his work with the church, Nader is a student at Jerusalem University in East Jerusalem, outside the Israeli checkpoints. But the intifada has put his education on hold.

"The semester began four months ago, but I am not able to attend classes regularly. Often I cannot reach the university. Even the teachers cannot reach the university. Nobody is allowed to walk on the streets there because of the curfew. I should be ready to graduate, but I am only in my third year."

But the curfews are not the only obstacles. Israeli roadblocks and checkpoints are constantly moved from one road to another.

"Every day we have to find a different way out of Ramallah. Sometimes we walk in the mountains. Sometimes in desert places. Sometimes through the checkpoint after waiting for a long time. Sometimes, after I have reached my destination, I cannot come back to Ramallah. I stay at my friend's house or try another way, another road. Today, it is open from one side, but maybe tomorrow it will be closed. It used to take 40 minutes to get to school. Now it can take many hours. And sometimes, you reach the checkpoint and they say 'Go back!'"

Nader spoke to us openly about the Israeli occupation of his town and the toll it is taking on the few believers trying to minister here. There was no anger or bitterness in his voice, although he was understandably very frustrated.

"In the past, many people from Jerusalem visited us. It was very encouraging to the church. We had conferences and meetings and could visit the churches in Jerusalem and Bethlehem. We were able to participate in Musalaha (a reconciliation ministry) with Jewish believers, where we could relate together as humans, as Christian believers, not as enemies. We and they are the Body of Christ.

"But now they have hard times in Israel and Jerusalem and we have hard times here. Now, there are no relations with other churches. We can only get word to them to pray for us."

In the hierarchy of suffering, children top the list.

Nader continued, "I have been working with children, teenagers and university students for five years. Over the past year of the intifada, they cannot feel that they are safe. The children are afraid. Everyday I hear that the children cannot go to school because they are crying, afraid that many things will happen to them. There is nothing on television but bad news.

"We have been trying to make the youth feel like everything is normal, as though nothing is happening, doing more activities to make them feel happy, to make them feel better. But you can see that their hearts are becoming more stony. Seeing blood all the time, their hearts are becoming hard."

Evangelical Palestinian Christians here hang on tightly to Romans 8:28, strengthening themselves and encouraging others with the conviction that "in all things God works for the good of those who love Him, who have been called according to His purpose." And they believe that he is able to build his kingdom, even out of the rubble of Ramallah.

"In spite of our troubles, the best time in my life has been the last year and a half," Nader admits with an engaging grin. "I can now walk through the streets and speak with the unbelieving youth. Because few people can get to work or to school, they have nothing to do, so you can speak with them about Christ.

"In the past, I used to go and visit them and they would say, 'No, we are busy. We cannot see you.' Now people are calling me and asking questions. Many of them feel that Christ is the only way to have a better life. And many are beginning to believe. Spiritually it is better, while physically it is more difficult. While we now have few conferences and attendance is low because of the intifada, the field is full of people.

"On the other hand, so many believers have left that we have no workers to visit the youth, answer their questions and encourage them. The few of us who are left are very busy. I have a list of people who have told me they would like to speak with me, but I do not have enough time to keep up with my studies and still speak to all of them."

Emigration is a significant problem for the historical churches as well as for the evangelical congregations. But with fewer than a hundred believers, compared to 10,000 tribal Christians, it is far more devastating for the evangelicals who find themselves caught in four-way crossfire.

Because they are Palestinian Arabs, they suffer at the hands of the Israeli army.

In addition, when they accept Christ and leave the Greek Orthodox or other historical churches, they also jeopardize their legal status.

"Without church here, you have no society," Labib explained. "The church in the Middle East is your security. It's not like the States.

"To register in a school, to get married or to be buried, you have to have your church certificate. To register with the government – both Israeli and Palestinian – you have to have your church certificate. Even atheists must belong to a church to have legal status. They just belong to a traditional, historical church.

"To the government, you are a Jew, a Muslim or a Christian. Whether you practice your faith or not is of no concern either to the Israeli government or to the Palestinian Authority (PA). It is simply part of your identity. If you are a Christian, you are Catholic, Orthodox or Protestant. Or you belong to an evangelical congregation."

Labib cited a recent example of humanitarian relief that never reached the families of evangelicals because they lack the powerful support structure of the Christian and Muslim organizations.

"The Arab Israelis in Galilee sent lorries full of food and other necessities for the Palestinians in Ramallah, both Muslims and Christians. Several Islamic organizations took responsibility for distribution to the Muslims. And the local Council of Churches – the traditional churches – took responsibility for dispersing food to the Christians. Some of the Evangelical leaders went to them and said, 'We're not Catholics. We're not Orthodox. We're not Anglicans. But we are still Christians, and we have families who need help.'

" 'Get out of here!,' they said. 'We don't recognize you.'"

"An Orthodox lady went to the Catholic priest," Nader added, "and just asked for milk for her child. He told her: 'Go to *your* church.' So you see the importance of the church in this country."

There remains a great gulf of misunderstanding between the historical and evangelical churches. In addition to being at odds with the Israelis and the traditional churches, believers in Palestine are virtually invisible to believers in the Western Church who could help to strengthen the struggling evangelical church in the Holy Land.

"We need prayer," Nader told us. "and we need a lot of people to help here. Many times, missionaries come from Egypt or other countries and start churches here. They stay for a while, but as soon as they leave, the church closes. There is no place here to train our own people to become pastors and leaders in the church. I used to go to Bethlehem Bible College, but I cannot reach it anymore.

"Years ago, I was the only male youth in the church. The pastor was in the United States, and there was no youth pastor. I needed other believers to talk to, and it was very difficult for me. There was no activity, nothing happening in the church. But it's better now."

Yesterday, however, Nader's current pastor left for the U.S., so it will be difficult again for this congregation.

We asked Labib and Nader what they saw as the greatest needs of the evangelical church in Palestine and how we as Western Christians can help meet those needs.

"I use the word 'adoption,'" Labib said. "You can not only help in the training, but also adopt and support those who are being trained, follow up on them, encourage them and love them."

Both agreed that one of the best ways to do this is through sister churches in the West – Christians and congregations willing to adopt a Palestinian congregation and help them fulfill their God-given call to reach their neighbors with the gospel of salvation and peace.

"If a believer in Ramallah or anywhere in Palestine has a gift for working with youth," Labib continued, "look for opportunities to train him. Western churches can consult with the local churches and ministries here. They can send him to the Bethlehem Bible College or to a college in Jordan, Egypt, England or the U.S. In addition to financial support, the Western church can give him desperately needed assurance that they are standing with him, that he is not alone.

"It is not all about financial support. Maybe some people can come and share their knowledge and skills. Teach puppetry for children's ministries. Teach music for praise and worship and outreach. Mobilize their churches to pray.

"Nader is a youth worker. Maybe two or three from a youth group in the West can come and stay for several days, just to sit and pray with him, encourage him and briefly share his daily life. It is mostly a fellowship thing. Brothers and sisters ministering to brothers and sisters, not the rich giving to the poor."

"We need to feel that we are part of the Body of Christ," Nader added. "We need strong relationships with other believers. The believers here feel that we are the only ones in the world. It's really hard. You feel lonely and fear for the future."

"You cannot imagine in the West," said Labib, "how much it would mean to an evangelical Palestinian Christian for you to say to him, 'God has purposes for your presence here. We want to see God's purposes fulfilled. We want to encourage you and stand with you.'"

"Wake up!" God told the church in Sardis in Revelation 3:2. "Strengthen what remains and is about to die." And He is saying the same thing today to the Western church concerning the church in the West Bank and Gaza.

If American Christians respond to this challenge, Labib said, it "will also enable the evangelical church to stand and give their members the legal cover that is required by the government. But if the church remains shaken and underdeveloped, the government says, 'Why should I recognize you? Who are you? Who is your pastor? Bring me a certificate from your pastor.' And the church has to hang its head and say, 'Sorry, he went for five months to the U.S.' Then the government says to the believers, 'Go back to your Catholic Church. Go back to your priests, you naughty boy. Get out of here!'"

"Another part of the problem for Palestinian believers," Nader said, "is that our neighbors see that we have relations with the U.S., and the U.S. is with Israel. So Palestinian evangelicals are perceived as being Zionist. The Muslims and traditional Christians say, 'You are evangelicals just like George Bush.'

"Last summer, there were some people from America who wanted to help here. The pastor told them, sorry we can't have you in our church because we'll have a problem with the Christian churches. So the Americans rented a house here in the city. Now they are perceived as helping in Ramallah instead of helping just in our church.

"Another time, some people in the U.S. provided us with Arabic tracts to help us reach out to the Muslims, but we could not distribute them because the tracts said they were printed in the U.S. You see the problem?

"It's all very dangerous. There are no police here now since the siege ended. The Palestinian police apparatus was destroyed by the Israelis. So if anyone accuses us of being with Israel, we will be killed. No one will help us."

We witnessed grisly evidence of this as we entered the town. A Palestinian accused of collaborating with the Israelis had been killed by a mob and hanged upside down from a tower in the center of the town square.

"In a recent mob attack," Nader said sadly, "rioters burned everything in their path. The police put officers in front of every church for protection – every church except the evangelical churches.

Linda Kasheshian

*   *   *   *

Linda Kasheshian (Kah-shesh'-ee-an) lives in Ramallah but attends the Alliance Church in the Old City of Jerusalem. She greeted us at the door, led us into a comfortable living room and disappeared briefly into the kitchen. Minutes later, she rejoined us, covering the coffee table with refreshments – a legendary, delicious and fattening Middle Eastern custom.

Linda knew Labib well, but Ron and I were strangers. As Americans, we stood out in Ramallah like a silo in a cornfield. But this gracious lady, with the warmth and charm of a Palestinian Aunt Bea, quickly put us at ease and settled in to answer our questions.

We began by asking Linda to share some of her background.

She said she was born into the Greek Orthodox Church but left sometime after an interesting encounter her father had with the Holy Spirit.

"One day, my father passed by a church and heard the message of salvation," she recalled. "He had a very bad headache that day and was going to the doctor. Instead, he went into the church and said, 'I want to try this God. If He heals me without going to the doctor, I will believe in Him.' And this is what happened. God healed him right away, and my father believed in Him.

"When my brother and sister and I were born, the Greek Orthodox wanted to baptize us as infants. But my father refused. He said, 'No, I want them to understand the new birth. Then let them ask for this baptism.' And he stood firm before all the priests. So when I was nine, the three of us were baptized in the River Jordan."

Her family left the Greek Orthodox Church and joined the Alliance Church where her father served as one of the elders who led the church, since it had no ordained pastor. After his death, Linda and another woman also became elders and helped lead the church.

"It was because of their service and faithfulness that the church survived until God sent another pastor," Labib said proudly. Labib too had served the Alliance Church as a lay pastor.

In addition to 37 years as an elementary school teacher, Linda teaches Sunday school and keeps the church accounts. Her husband, Ramez, is also a believer and works at a hotel in Jerusalem. They have two sons.

"My children were an answer from the Lord," says Linda, beaming. "The first came after six years of marriage. The Lord promised to give me one, so I was waiting for His promise to be fulfilled. My other son came four years later. They love the Lord, and one of them is still here. He serves in the church in Jerusalem by recording the worship and messages every Sunday. My other son is studying computer science in St. Louis."

Talking about her family reminded Linda of the recently ended siege.

"For three weeks, I was praying that God would protect and help us. And He was faithful. Israeli soldiers were going from house to house, looking for wanted persons and weapons. They took many of the youth, young boys, but not my son.

"Fifteen soldiers came to our house. They banged loudly at the back door, and I told them to go around to the front door, that we don't use the back door because it is difficult to open. But they kept shouting, and my son helped me to open it. They made him walk ahead of them as one soldier pointed his gun toward my son's back and another pointed his gun at his side. The others went from room to room, searching for weapons, and of course, we don't have any. Then they left.

"In the afternoon, they lifted the curfew briefly, and I went with my son to look for bread. It was a great shock to us. Ramallah looked as if an earthquake took place. The streets were all dirty from the tanks. There were many ditches and lots of damage. Electrical poles, telephone boxes, shops, traffic lights, signs, buildings, sidewalks. There were tens of smashed cars. The tanks broke the wall at the entrance to our house and pushed our neighbor's van up the side. She had to pay 400 shekels (US$100) to rent a winch to put it back on the ground, and she still waits to have it repaired.

"The curfew was very strict. We were not allowed to get rid of our trash in the municipal containers outside our houses. We could not get anything off our balconies, for if we opened the doors, we might be shot. Soldiers were scattered on the tops of buildings and shot at anything that moved. The Israelis lifted the curfew for about two hours at a time. People hurried, mainly to buy bread and medicine and milk for their children. No one knew if the milk or other perishable foods were still good, because many areas were without electricity.

"One morning, at 3 A.M., the soldiers came to my house again and knocked at my door. I was alone. My son had gotten out of the city and gone to Jerusalem when the Israelis briefly lifted the curfew.

" 'Who's there?' I called.

" 'Soldiers,' they shouted. 'Open the door!'

"I went to the door and opened it. They came in and asked who else was in the house. I told them that my husband and my son were in Jerusalem and I was here by myself. They searched the rooms. They searched my son's room. They asked me to go out to open the storage shed in the back. Then they told me to go back into the house, close the door and turn off the lights.

"Next, they went to my neighbor's house. She can hear nothing without her hearing aid. So I was by the window, looking at her door, praying that they wouldn't explode the door. They went to the next neighbor, then came back and knocked again. I told them that she can't hear, that she takes off her hearing aid at night. The other neighbor told them the same thing. And I prayed that they would believe us and leave. They knocked the third time, and she still didn't hear them. I prayed more that they would not explode the door. And God heard, and they left.

"Without the Lord, I could never have made it. It's really fearful when you see fifteen soldiers surrounding you. I was most afraid at night. We don't have any shelters to hide in when they throw bombs or shoot. I would just stand in the hallway and pray for God's protection.

"We couldn't even sleep many nights because of the heavy tanks. You feel them as if they are driving on top of your house. They make a big, big noise. And the shooting never stops."

When the soldiers lifted the curfew, thousands of people poured out of their homes into the streets, wide-eyed as they walked through the rubble. Pale and weak from fear, lack of sleep and rationing of food supplies. Some helped one another. Others cared only for their own needs. Shopping was frenzied at shops and markets as families tried to get what supplies they could to last until the next brief break in the curfew.

"We know a family of Christian believers here in Ramallah whose two sons were taken by the Israeli soldiers. The father was crying in the street. They took his sons for several days, and I encouraged the father to pray. 'Your sons are innocent,' I told him, 'so they will be released.' Thank God, they were finally sent home.

"Once, when they lifted the curfew, I met a mother and a girl. She's in grade five; I taught her in grade three. And she was crying in the street. I asked why she was crying, and the mother told me, 'We live near Arafat's headquarters, and our house has been completely destroyed.' She was going to stay with her grandmother in a different area."

While the intifada has been very difficult for Linda and her family, she, like Nader, feels worst for the children.

"The children don't have a chance to live their childhood. All they think of is the intifada. They're worried. Whenever they write something in their copybooks, they mention the intifada. They draw only Israeli tanks and soldiers, bullets, fighting. We even see that they fight with each other more, because they are being brought up during the intifada. They don't know any other life.

"Before this current intifada, we used to take the children on educational field trips to Nablus and Jericho, places in their textbooks. But we can't take them anymore. And they keep asking us, 'Please take us on trips.'

" 'Where do you want to go?' we ask. And they say, 'to the ice-cream shop.' They consider a visit to something only five minutes away from the school as a *trip*, because they don't remember what trips really are.

"Today, before you came, we were told at the school that the parents are coming to take their children. We heard that the Israeli's are again going to occupy Ramallah in retaliation for the latest suicide bombing, and they were taking their children home.

The children are living a very difficult life."

But Linda too sees God's hand at work in Ramallah despite the bloody intifada.

"More people have started praying. They are giving more thought to God. A Christian friend told me when they took the Church of the Nativity in Bethlehem, she was praying all the time that the people inside the church might come to know God through this difficulty. And I was praying with her. We have been praying for different families in Bethlehem, in Ramallah, in Nablus. There are believers all over the area, and we have been praying for one another."

What it would be like without the impassioned prayers of the saints, Linda cannot imagine.

"I thank God that my telephone kept on working. Many people lost telephone service the minute the Israelis entered the city. My sister didn't have electricity for eight days. Some people were without food and water.

"We hear of more people stealing in the city because they don't have money. Many workers lost their jobs. My son works in a factory. Recently, they told him that he needed to get a special new identity card to continue to work there. With the Israeli occupation, it took him two weeks to get the card, and when he returned to the factory, his job was gone.

"I have a relative in Bethlehem whose husband whitewashes houses. But nobody whitewashes or cleans or paints anymore with all of the shelling. They don't have money. Once I was able to send money through her father, but now he cannot get to Bethlehem to take her money.

"Some neighbors told me that the soldiers cut their furniture open with knives looking for weapons. Of course, lots of windows were broken from bombing and shelling and shooting. Many people died, especially in Ramallah. Ambulances were not able to get to the injured people and take them to the hospital. In the Ramallah Hospital, we had 29 bodies, and they were not allowed to bury them or give them to their families. Instead, when the

Israelis lifted the curfew, they dug a big hole in the hospital garden and buried all of them together.

"The soldiers damaged many other buildings. If they were military buildings, we could understand. But they were homes and shops that belonged to civilians, to people who didn't do any harm. Still their places were damaged.

"After the soldiers left, the youth, all the scouts, students, municipality members, even the mayor, went to the streets with brooms, sweeping, sweeping, sweeping the damage, the glass, the rubble in the streets.

"Many people lost their cars, houses, money. We thank God for some believers who are sending money. I received a gift last week and was able to help six families to buy basic food."

We asked how all of this made Linda feel and whether her emotions conflict with her Christianity.

"I never hated anybody in my life, even the Jews. But I hate what they do sometimes. Sometimes I get mad when they go in and kill for nothing. They keep accusing us of being terrorists. But what about what they are doing to us? I sent many emails during the curfew — to 16 different people in England and America, and they shared them in their churches. I thank them all, because they were praying for all the believers here. I kept writing to tell them that we also are victims. Some of them answered back and said, 'We never heard of Palestinian victims. We always hear that you are terrorists. Now we can understand.'"

"Sometimes my cousin asks, 'Where *is* your God?'

" 'He is here,' I answer. 'He has a reason. His thoughts are not like our thoughts. His ways are not our ways.'

" 'No,' he says, 'your God loves only the Jews! He is turning his face completely from us. We keep praying. We keep praying. And nobody answers.'

"Even the principal of my school told me, 'Maybe God is fed up with all our prayers. He doesn't want to listen to us anymore. People pray and pray and pray, and they see nothing change. Why are we praying to God? Where is God? He's not listening to us.'

"But I know God is here and He protects and He takes care of us."

*   *   *   *

The sensation as we drove back into West Jerusalem from Ramallah was like flying in a jetliner through dark, boiling thunderclouds into clear blue skies.

We parked and took the elevator to the offices of Musalaha where we were to meet Dr. Salim J. Munayer (Sah-leem' Moon'-ah-yer), the ministry founder.

Musalaha (Moo-sah'-la-ha) is Arabic for forgiveness and reconciliation. It is a ministry that brings together Jew and Arab, Israeli and Palestinian so they can see one another as fellow men and women, families just like theirs – not as "the enemy."

Its literature describes Musalaha as "a ministry that seeks to expand reconciliation between Palestinian Arabs and Israeli Jews according to scriptural principles. The central theme is Jesus' atonement on the cross and His resurrection as the only hope through which this can be accomplished. We seek to be a model, an encouragement and a facilitator of reconciliation."

Salim Munayer was born in the city of Lod, about 30 miles southeast of Tel Aviv, a city that was inhabited mostly by Palestinian Christians and Muslims. In 1948, when the city was conquered by the Israeli army, most of the people were driven out.

"My parents went at that time to hide in the church," Salim explained, "and they were able to stay in the city. Only 200 Christians were left. The rest became refugees. Jews from all around the world moved there and lived first in the empty Arab houses. Then new neighborhoods were built."

As a result, Salim grew up in a mixed city, knowing Hebrew and Arabic, knowing the Jewish and Palestinian culture, aware of the tension and the difficulties.

"When I was old enough to enter high school, my parents had to choose whether to send me to Nazareth to dormitory school or to send me next door to the Jewish high school. So they sent me to the Hebrew high school because it was more affordable.

"In addition to my academic subjects, I was taught all the bad things that Christians did to Jews in Europe. We also studied about Stalin, Lenin, Hitler, Churchill and Mao and the philosophers. But when I asked my Jewish teacher, what about Jesus, we ended up in an argument. I lost the argument because he was better educated than I.

Salim and Kay Munayer with their sons. In addition to being founder and president of Musalaha, Salim serves as Academic Dean for Bethlehem Bible College.

"One day, my uncle, who is a believer, put an ad in *The Jerusalem Post*, asking who would be willing to teach the New Testament. He was very much concerned that the boys and girls in our family would grow up hearing only the Israeli side but would not also know the New Testament.

"A Jewish believer answered the ad. So every Friday at his

home we had a Bible study. Jews from my school who wanted to know more about Jesus also came. From the beginning, my encounter with the Lord was in the context of Jews and Arabs studying the New Testament together.

"At 22, I became a believer and saw that Jesus is the only answer for both Arabs and Jews. That was when I first began to recognize the solution to our problems here in terms of forgiveness and reconciliation."

Salim came to the United States and attended Fuller Theological Seminary School of World Missions in California. By the time he had earned his master's degree, Israel had changed dramatically.

"When I came back, I started teaching at Bethlehem Bible College, where I saw firsthand how people are forced to live in the West Bank and Gaza. You don't see it on TV. And even though you may read about it in a few books, you cannot really understand what it is like day after day under the occupation until you have lived with the people. Then you see clearly that the situation is leading to a terrible explosion."

It wasn't long before the first intifada erupted.

"On December 8, 1987, in an incident that ignited much popular tension, four Palestinians were killed in a traffic accident in the Gaza Strip. Rumors quickly spread that this was not an accident but a deliberate attempt to kill Palestinians. The next day, young Palestinians were on the streets confronting Israeli soldiers with nothing more than stones. Responding to rocks with gunfire, the soldiers shot and killed a 15-year-old boy who became the first martyr of the Intifada. The rage of Palestinians grew, and the Intifada soon spread to every town and village in the West Bank and Gaza Strip." [2]

Within the first 12 months, 311 Palestinians had been killed and 6,000 placed in detention camps.

The people of Beit Sahour (Bet Sah-hoor'), however, while having their share of rock-throwing shebab, collectively decided upon a non-violent approach. At a small village in the Bethlehem area, its citizens launched a citywide tax revolt that threatened to spread and seriously damage the fragile Israeli economy. But Israel saw to it that the revolt never left the city.

> "On September 19, 1989, the Israeli army entered Beit Sahour with hundreds of troops and imposed a strict military curfew. They cut phone lines and barred the press and the Israeli solidarity groups from entering. Beit Sahour was under complete siege. Soldiers went from house to house and business to business, confiscating truckloads of goods. An estimated $2 million worth of commercial equipment and personal property, including televisions, stoves, refrigerators, furniture, medicine from pharmacies, and factory machinery were taken by force to compensate for unpaid taxes. All of the produce and canned goods were stripped from the shelves of the main grocery store in town. . . . On November 1, after 42 days, the siege was finally lifted, but Beit Sahour defiantly continued its resistance, in part because it had no choice. It could not afford to turn back, given the exorbitant fines and back taxes that the Israelis were demanding. The town leaders announced a hundred-day general strike, and shops remained closed through February 1990 to protest the siege." [3]

Neither violence nor non-violence has succeeded in resolving the conflict in the Middle East. The gospel is the only hope, not only for unbelievers but for believers as well.

"In 1989," Salim said, "we realized that the issue of reconciliation is essential in the gospel. We cannot just have an annual gathering of believers, praise the Lord and think that we have dealt with the issue. Reconciliation needs ongoing ministry to deal with the fundamental issues that separate us. There are offenses on both sides, so the solution requires a fundamental heart change of the people of both sides. It's not just a compromise, because the margin of compromise is very limited here. So I called leaders among both Arab and Jewish believers and we established Musalaha."

Musalaha is based upon several fundamental principles. The first is man's need for relationship.

"A very important scripture for us here is 1 John 4, especially verse 20:

> If anyone says, "I love God," yet hates his brother, he is a liar. For anyone who does not love his brother, whom he has seen, cannot love God, whom he has not seen.

"The test of our spirituality, of our being disciples of Jesus, has to be our relationship with each other.

"The second principle is found in Ephesians 2, which details what Jesus did on the cross. He became our peace. He made Jew and non-Jew one. He destroyed the barriers and the dividing wall of hostility. So the aspect of the cross is for us essential. This is where we all agree that without the cross, there is no reconciliation to God and no reconciliation to one another.

"The final principle is our proclamation, who we are to our community. This is found in John 17:20-21:

> I pray also for those who will believe in me through their message, that all of them may be

one, Father, just as you are in me and I am in
you. May they also be in us so that the world
may believe that you have sent me.

"Jesus' identity and character is manifest when an Arab and a
Jew reconcile with one another. And that must be our declaration
to our community."

All of this makes a great sermon, Salim admitted, but the hard
part is putting these principles into action.

"To have a relationship, we first have to deal with the dehumanization of our community. That means dealing with presuppositions that both Israelis and Palestinians have. These
presuppositions are the result of wars, hurt, loss, the education of
the culture and the conflict within the community. The average
Israeli or Palestinian boy, by age five, has a very clear image of who
is the enemy. This becomes part of our core identity and has to be
dealt with.

"Dehumanization and demonization occur when we justify
what we are and what we do in the name of God. In the name of
God, we are doing the most terrible things to each other, to people
who have been created in His image and likeness. And in the
process we demonize those whom we dehumanize."

Launching relationships between Arabs and Jews, however, is
extremely difficult in Israel, particularly during intifada. So Salim
and the Musalaha leadership were forced to look for more neutral
ground.

"We found that the best way is to take groups of Arabs and
Jews into the desert. In most cases, apart from the desert experience, when Israeli and Palestinian met with each other, they immediately entered into arguments and accusations of who started the
conflict, whose fault, whose right to the land, and so on that are
not pleasing to God.

"So we go for five days into the desert on camels. The desert
forces people indirectly to deal with several issues. First, the
desert is a trial of faith. It is a place where you don't play games.

"Usually, they are so afraid of the camels that they are distracted from talking about politics."

No longer surrounded by cultural reminders of their differences, Arab and Jewish believers are able to relate to one another as fellow human beings and members of the body of Christ.

The desert is a place where the prophets went to meet with God. It is a place where we realize how great He is and how small we are. But more than anything else, if we are not going to be united, we are not going to survive.

"So we put on each camel an Israeli and a Palestinian – one riding and one leading the camel. The whole experience really breaks the dehumanization and demonization and enables people to enter into a relationship. Then they get to know each other and start talking about the issues.

"In the desert, we sit together and we worship the Lord in Arabic and Hebrew. And we found that amazingly important, because the language of the enemy suddenly is the language in which you hear him worshiping God. We are currently publishing a worship book in Arabic, Hebrew and English, so people who don't know one another's language can worship the Lord together."

The desert experience, however, is just the beginning. Like faith, a new relationship must be tested in order to endure and mature.

"Immediately when they come back from the desert, there is pressure from their communities to return to their old way of thinking and to prove their tribal loyalty. So we have monthly or bimonthly follow-up programs to reinforce what they have discovered and to deepen their relationships, learning each other's history, keeping open the lines of communication in order to complete the reconciliation process."

Musalaha has several "tracks." One focuses on leaders, another on students, and others on women and families. For the most part, the ministry works with believers.

"We started with believers only because believers have a biblical mandate to be agents of peace – biblical peace, not political peace, the peace of God. We are commanded to be peacemakers. We are commanded to love our enemies, to fight evil with good. If Christian believers cannot be agents of peace here in the land, we dilute our faith and the message of the cross.

"We also work with some nonbelievers. Actually, it is sometimes easier to work with nonbelievers than with believers.
Believers are a minority and they feel that they want to prove their
loyalty to their group, whether Jew or Arab. As a result, they
often take an even stronger nationalistic position. On the other
hand, believers understand the spiritual dimension. How much
you love God, how close you are to God, determines how much
you are able to reconcile with your brother.

"Minority groups like evangelical Palestinian Christians feel a
stronger need for reconciliation than majority groups like traditional Christians, Jews or Muslims. In America, for instance, Black
people have a stronger need for reconciliation than white people,
because Black people feel the tension more than the white. Here,
the Palestinian Christian believer is often more anxious for reconciliation than the Israeli believer. When you reconcile with your
brother, there is a changing of power. You are looking one another
in the eye. That is uncomfortable for the majority group that has
the power, and it changes the way each group sees itself. The
majority group had perceived itself as just and fair and open-
minded. Suddenly it realizes that it is behaving unjustly, with bias
and bigotry."

In some ways, the leadership and youth events are the most
strategic because the former are the vanguard into the future while
the latter *are* the future.

"At a recent leadership conference," Salim recalled, "the Lord
moved upon our hearts. Leaders were standing up and confessing
that they served in the army during the current conflict and that
they did terrible things. Then they asked God and their brothers
and sisters to forgive them.

"We had to come together before we were able to realize that
the level of bitterness, hatred, revenge and retaliation had become
a block in our relationship to God. If we had not sat together, we
would not have realized how polluted our hearts had become. But
we stood and we confessed and we wept. It was like a bath, a
cleansing. And we were able to move forward.

Labib, his wife Caroline and their children attended a recent

Musalaha leadership conference held in Holland and learned as much from the children as from the adults.

"At the end of one day," Labib recalled, "I was taking my son Matthew up to the room. I gave him something, and he looked at me and said, *to'da*, which is 'thank you' in Hebrew. My son knows some English and some Arabic, but he has never learned any Hebrew words at all, nothing. Just playing around with the other children – Israelis and Palestinians – he picked it up. It was just a little word he learned, but it meant so much to me. A little Arab boy, and without even thinking, it came naturally to him to say to me thank you in Hebrew.

"Every day, the parents gathered just to watch our children playing together, and you could not tell who was who. They were just a group of kids. We looked at that picture and we said, 'This is the future we want.'"

To grasp the impact these children really had on their Israeli and Palestinian parents, it is important to understand what it is like to grow up in Israel or in the occupied lands.

"In high schools today, it's awful what's going on," Salim explained. "The level of hatred is unbelievable. You know, there is enough reason to hate. There is no need for more to come from teachers and textbooks. The reality of life is enough. Most schools just don't deal with the issues and by omission, they reinforce the hatred.

"Israeli and Palestinian youth grow up on totally separate tracks. They don't meet with each other. For many of the youth, the desert is the first time they have ever met with anyone from the other side, the first time they talk and realize that they share the same needs, goals, challenges and dreams."

As with other Musalaha groups, follow-up with students and youth is vital.

"We often challenge them to do social work in each other's community, because there is a wall of fear of visiting these communities. By doing social work there, we empower them to break the wall of fear. It is like going out of the camp and back in and being a witness to both communities.

"One of the most powerful follow-up events is learning about one another's histories, seeing events from the other person's perspective, walking in one another's shoes.

"We don't compare experiences. We simply say, your neighbors went through this traumatic experience that affected them very much. For example, we bring in people or immediate family of those who have been casualties in the current situation, like a Palestinian man whose father was shot by the Israelis. We went to his home. He told his story and we prayed together. Then we went to the site of a suicide bombing on Ben Yehuda Street. A believer who was almost killed there told her story, and we prayed with her."

Evan Thomas, a Jewish believer from New Zealand, pastor of Beit Asaf Messianic Congregation in the coastal city of Netanya and a member of the Musalaha Board of Directors, emotionally recalls one such event.

"In early November 1995, while on a Musalaha trip to Jordan with a mixed group of Palestinian Christians and Messianic Jews, a unique task was placed on my heart by the Lord. And that was to facilitate a visit to the Holocaust Museum, *Yad Vashem,* with a small selected group of leaders from our respective communities. I sensed the concept was deeply rooted in the words of the Apostle Paul to the Galatians: 'Bear one another's burdens, and thus fulfill the law of Jesus' (Galatians 6:2).

"Yad Vashem and the memory of the Holocaust are intrinsic to our very identities as Israelis and inseparable from the foundations of the state. They form a part of the education of our children and each year are marked by memorial ceremonies. Nearly every Messianic congregation has second or third generation sufferers of Holocaust survivor's syndrome and many of us have knowledge of our own family members who perished in the Nazi camps.

"Aware of prevailing political sentiment towards Yad Vashem, I knew that very few of my Palestinian colleagues had ever visited the site. I somehow felt that in order to truly know me as a Jewish brother, to accompany me would be very helpful and exhibit a deep mark of trust. I decided to evaluate the 'raw concept' with one of the participants on the Jordan trip, Alex Awad (pastor of an Arab Baptist congregation in Jerusalem and teacher at Bethlehem Bible College). He patiently listened to me and responded positively, though warning me of the cultural and community sensitivities that were involved.

"To give it balance he had a valuable suggestion to make – to consider also including a visit by the same group to a modern historical site of Palestinian suffering.

"So, on November 5, 1997, a group of us (five Palestinian and three Israeli believers) met in an outer suburb of Jerusalem called *Har Nof* – the site of the village of *Deir Yassin*. Today the neighborhood is predominantly religious and dotted with *yeshivot* (religious training schools) and all that is left of the original village is the beautifully preserved central part, now functioning as a mental institution.

"We stood on the busy street in the steady rain listening attentively to our Palestinian brothers recount the terrible events of the Deir Yassin massacre. Often they would refer to books written by Israeli historians.

"In brief, history reflects that in 1948, just prior to the establishment of our state and only three years after the Holocaust, paramilitary troops of the *Irgun* surrounded the village. A decision had been made that in order to capture and hold Jerusalem; it would be essential to first capture and completely clear the village of Deir Yassin and its nearby neighborhoods for their strategic significance. At dawn the troops moved in and completed the task, and in so doing approximately 250 men, women, and children lost their lives. Records show that bodies were mutilated and women raped and the village completely ransacked and cleared as ordered. Some of the surviving men were rounded up and driven by truck to other villages in the area and allowed to tell what had happened. The resulting panic caused these villagers to turn to flee out of fear. The men were then once more rounded up and executed. From the point of view of the Irgun, the operation was a total success.

"Our Palestinian brothers shared their pain of these terrible memories. Two brothers who were with us, Alex and Bishara, had been nine and eleven years old at the time and had just prior to the massacre lost their father, shot down by an unknown gunman in front of the family home. As a result they were placed in a boarding school. The surviving children of the village of Deir Yassin were to join them, and their horror became their nightmare.

"My Israeli counterparts and I were deeply moved by our brothers' sadness and vulnerability and were able to identify with the shame and sin of our countrymen, realizing that these men, within three years of the Holocaust were committing the same dreadful acts that they themselves had been victims of. The abused had quickly become the abusers.

"Moving up into the village center, we stopped at a junction in the narrow streets and under overcast skies, lifted before the Lord this terrible event that mars our common history. As we prayed together in tears, we were able to look at one another in a different way. It was as though something had been aired and cleared between us.

"Following some refreshments together, we made the short journey to the Holocaust museum. Prior to entering the building, the tension and nervousness was very evident among the Palestinians. I took the time to reassure them once again of the non-political motives behind this visit, and we committed this stage of our journey to the Lord in prayer. As we walked slowly through the corridors of photograph displays and historical testimony, our brothers were deeply moved and overawed at the scale of the atrocities. It was very difficult to take it all in.

"From the museum we moved up into the Hall of Names. Here two million names of victims are recorded. One of the Israeli Messianic Jews accompanying us, Asher Intrater, handed the young woman sitting behind one of the computers the name of one of his family members, known to have perished in the Nazi conquest of Poland. As we gathered around him, the information began to emerge, revealing 39 family members from the same region who had died in the death camps. This, for all of us, made it very personal and once again, we were drawn very close to one another via the intimacy of these painful memories.

"Coming out into the fresh air, we took time to express what was going on within our hearts. We were very careful not to draw comparisons between the events of the Holocaust and Deir Yassin, the dissimilarities of scale and implications being too vast. But it was important to see them in the context of their effects on our respective communities and on our own identities. We joined hands and, in Hebrew and Arabic, offered to the Lord the same prayer he taught his first disciples, 'Our Father which art in Heaven . . . .'" [4]

Despite stories like these, Salim said sadly, "the more common response to the idea of reconciliation has been to scoff."

Forgiveness and reconciliation are foreign concepts both to Judaism and to Islam.

"To Jews, forgiveness sounds too much like forgetfulness. To Muslims, forgiveness sounds too much like giving up and relinquishing their claims." [5]

"It is not a popular idea," Salim continued. "Those who seek relationships with the other, or the 'enemy,' rarely receive the praise of their own people. There is the sense that those who meet with the other side betray or undermine the interests and identities of their own. Suspicions are high. Anger is rampant. Trust is lost. For many, this is not the time to reconcile; this is the time to protect.

"In addition to these obstacles, Musalaha must navigate the logistical obstacles of bringing Palestinians and Israelis together. Travel and location have become difficult issues. Some are afraid to go to certain places. Some are prohibited from leaving or entering areas and unable to cross checkpoints.

"Nevertheless, believers continue, in spite of tremendous pressure, to come together, to try to help each other and to embrace one another.

"This is evidence of two things. First, God's Spirit is alive and at work among believers here. And second, believers are being obedient to His command to be members of the body of the Jesus, the Messiah.

"As 1 Corinthians 12:24-27 states:

> God has combined the members of the body and has given greater honor to the parts that lacked it, so that there should be no division in the body, but that its parts should have equal concern for each other. If one part suffers, every part suffers with it; if one part is honored, every part rejoices with it. Now you are the body of Christ, and each one of you is part of it."

*   *   *   *

Back in our hotel rooms, we caught up on the news of the day.

ITEM: The Israeli Security Cabinet is expected tonight to approve a military incursion into the Gaza Strip in retaliation for the suicide bombing in Rishon Lezion. Gaza is the home base of Hamas. We are told that the government is already calling up the reserves. Will we be able to get into Gaza tomorrow? If not, we will try to enter Bethlehem.

ITEM: Downtown, more than 10,000 Israelis have gathered for the Jerusalem Day parade, despite the fact that it is a prime target for a major terrorist attack. Sharing this concern, Palestinian Authority Chairman Arafat read a statement on Palestinian TV tonight ordering his security forces to prevent any terrorist operations.

We were awakened about 2:30 A.M. by what sounded like the thud of a bomb and the crack of rifle fire. Our hotel is very close to Hadasseh Hospital on Mount Scopus, where Jerusalem suicide bombing victims are taken. So our first reaction was to listen for sirens. There were none, and we quickly discovered that the noise was a Jerusalem Day fireworks display.

It doesn't take long before even visitors fall into the terrible rhythm of intifada.

Notes

[1] Matthew Gutman, "What in God's name am I doing here?" (*The Jerusalem Post*, Monday, May 20, 2002).

[2] Alex Awad, *Through the Eyes of the Victims* (Bethlehem Bible College, Bethlehem, October 2001), pp. 38-39.

[3] Charles M. Sennott, *The Body and the Blood* (Public Affairs, New York, 2001), pp. 157-158.

[4] Salim J. Munayer, *Seeking and Pursuing Peace: The Process, the Pain, and the Product* (Musalaha, Jerusalem, 1998), pp. 155-158, *reprinted by permission.*

[5] Charles M. Sennott, ibid, p. 431.

May 9

Hatred stirs up dissension, but love covers over all wrongs. Proverbs 10:12

This is the third time Israeli tanks have entered Bethlehem in
less than six months. For nearly six weeks, the Church of the
Nativity had been under siege. Israeli soldiers strictly enforce a
24-hour curfew. Anyone found outside at any time for any reason
risks being shot.

There were five of us in the car, two Americans and three
Palestinians, including Rev. Alex Awad, co-founder of Bethlehem
Bible College and pastor of East Jerusalem Baptist Church.

The Israeli checkpoint was littered with debris and bristled
with tanks, massive armored bulldozers and personnel carriers.
We slowed, but no one approached the car. So we rolled cau-
tiously through, praising God for enabling us to get in.

Three hundred yards down the road, we passed a concrete
machine gun emplacement at an intersection.

"Hey!" yelled a voice from the bunker.

We stopped and backed up, while tanks and other armored
vehicles swung around us from several directions.

An Israeli soldier looked down at us. He asked who we were
and what we were doing. I rolled down the car window and called
up to him. I said we were bringing humanitarian aid to the
Bethlehem Bible College, including some food for a couple of
Buddhist monks who had come to pray during the siege and were
now holed up at the college. All true.

The armed teenager was polite. He radioed the checkpoint, then called down again to me. Yelling back and forth from the car to his high concrete perch with the roar of engines and the thunder of tanks proved impossible. So I got out, smiling up at him and keeping both hands where he could see them.

After several discussions with the checkpoint, he said, "You'll have to go back. Sorry. Rules." I got back into the car, and we turned around.

At the checkpoint, we were told curtly that we would not be allowed in.

So we did what all Palestinians do under such circumstances. We headed for the mountains to find a back way into Bethlehem, calling ahead by cell phone to ask someone to meet us.

The car stopped on a dusty road, and we continued on foot. Over a hill, we met our contact, Rev. Nihad Salman (Nee-hahd' Sahl'-mahn), pastor of Emmanuel Evangelical Church, who was risking his life to take us to the college. We stuffed ourselves into his four-door compact and proceeded into Bethlehem through Beit Jala, a small suburb.

Minutes later, we passed Pastor Nihad's house, its ground floor windows packed with sandbags, its walls pockmarked with .50 caliber bullet holes – some cemented over, others fresh. In the distance, a white IDF blimp with a spy camera in its belly hovered over the Church of the Nativity.

We continued slowly through the deserted streets of Bethlehem. At every corner, Pastor Nihad paused, looked for soldiers and listened for the clanking treads of the more than 150 tanks patrolling the city. If we were seen in the streets during curfew, the soldiers would not ask for passports or explanations. We would be given no opportunity to convince them that we were not terrorists, that the car was not packed with explosives. It would be over in seconds.

Chunks of concrete were everywhere. Skeletons of cars lay twisted and charred. Trash uncollected for more than a month smoldered in a field. Pasted on doors and walls were color posters of those whom the Palestinians considered martyrs. Faces of adults and children killed in the conflict stared at us as we drove through narrow alleys, down a stony hill and across a field into a tiny parking area behind the college. The building sits on a hill with the front at street level and the back even with the basement.

Moments after we left the car, a 50-ton Merkeva tank mounted with a 105 mm gun thundered over our heads, and we stepped gratefully inside the cool, ancient walls.

Even buildings, however, offer little protection during a military incursion.

Bethlehem Bible College sustained extensive damage the previous Easter. The central electrical board was shot up, cutting off electricity and communications. Rooftop water tanks were punctured, solar panels were cracked and boilers damaged. Tank fire also burst water pipes and shattered 67 windows.

One evening, after teaching her English class, Samia Ata (Sahme'-ah Ah'-tah) left the college for home. The streets were empty and quiet. All the students had gone. A young man stood in the doorway of the shop next door. Samia walked to her car which she had parked on the sidewalk at the college entrance.

According to college president, Dr. Bishara Awad (Bi-shah'-ra Ah-wahd'), "Samia reached out to fit the key in into the lock of the car door when a whistling shriek split the air. A fraction of a second later, a shell exploded against the doorway of the shop, scattering thousands of sharp stone chips and other debris. For a moment she stood frozen in shock, not understanding what had happened. Then, looking down, she saw blood gushing from her right foot and realized she had been hit. She nearly lost consciousness from the sight and started screaming in panic for help. No one was at the college to respond to her cries, so she managed, in an act of sheer will, to unlock her car and drive to the convent clinic up the hill from the college.

"Several shrapnel fragments had to be removed from her right calf, ankle and foot. However, at least two fragments were left in place since, according to the doctors, their removal could cause complications including nerve and tissue damage radiating up to the hip and lower back."

Bethlehem Bible College was founded in 1979 by Bishara Awad and his brother, Alex. It's mission statement is to "train Christian leaders for service in the Arabic-speaking churches in Palestine, Israel and throughout the Arab world."

From left: Dr. Bishara Awad, Rev. Alex Awad and Rev. Nihad Salman.

One hundred thirty-five students, on average, attend the college, whose 35,000-volume library serves as the only public library in Bethlehem. Bachelor's degrees are available in General Education, Bible, Christian Education and Christian Counseling, with minors in music and history/archeology. Its unique Tour Guide Program provides students with 609 hours of study in addition to field trips. And the BBC Choir has performed worldwide, including tours in the United States, the UK, Scandinavia and Germany.

Unfortunately, the college recently was forced to suspend its

International Students Program, due to the instability of the political situation.

We walked upstairs to the main floor and into Bishara's office, where we shared a meal out of some of the provisions we had brought.

For the next hour, Bishara, Alex and Nihad discussed their perspective, both as evangelical Christians and as Palestinians:

"We never thought we would be under siege, under curfew this long," Bishara said. "Everyday we receive false hopes. Everyday, they say maybe, maybe."

The men also shared heartbreaking examples of injustice.

One was of a "Christian man named Thabet from Ramallah whose daughter, a young lady, was eating an orange, and she choked. She couldn't breathe. The father wanted to take her to the hospital, but every time he would step out of the house, the soldiers would shout, 'Go back in! Go back in!' and threatened to shoot him. He said 'Please, I want to go to the hospital.' No way. They did not let him go out. And so he called the Red Cross, he called the ambulances, but nobody could reach him. The young lady died. For three days, he couldn't bury her. Finally, he and his wife took her out in the garden and dug a hole and buried her.

"The same story of a doctor with his small child with asthma. The baby had severe attacks, and the doctor could not save the baby. They could not bury the baby. He and his wife also went out in the garden at night and buried their child."

Alex walked over to a filing cabinet and took down a color poster like the thousands we had seen pasted on walls as we drove into the city. He unrolled it and held it open for us to see. The writing was in Arabic. The photograph was of a handsome man, perhaps in his mid-thirties or early-forties, wearing a blue suit coat and blue sweater.

Alex: "Achmed Norman, a Muslim, runs the hospital. During the curfew, he got written permission from the Israelis to go to the hospital. And they told him to wear white so the soldiers would know that he was a doctor. They asked for the color and license plate number of his car, and said, 'You can go.' But when he went out, the soldiers opened fire. So he went back to his house and called the Israelis and said, 'They are shooting at my car.' And the Israelis said, 'Okay, this time put a sign or something like that in your car.' So he went out the second time, and they shot him in his head. We knew this doctor very well."

Bishara: "Every time there is a problem here – and there have been five wars already, beside all the intifadas and now the siege, Christians just give up, pack and leave. This is my concern and that of every Christian leader here, that Bethlehem and the Holy Land will be left with no Christians."

Historically, the Christian presence in Israel, the West Bank and Gaza Strip has dropped from between 13 and 20 percent in the early twentieth century to an estimated 1.5 percent today.[1]

According to Israeli officials, 2,766 Palestinian Christians emigrated from the West Bank in the first year of the current intifada. About 1,640 were from the Bethlehem area.[2]

Alex: "Bishara and I come from a family of seven brothers and sisters. We are the only two here. My mother, brothers and sisters, uncles, they all have left and are living in America and Germany. This is just one example. Some families have been completely wiped out of the Holy Land."

Nihad: "And once they leave, they leave for good. There are no jobs here, no security, no development. If they get educated, they have no jobs where they can use their education. In the place where Christianity started, the Christians are leaving."

Alex: "The church once flourished here. Now the church is dying here. But Western Christians don't seem to care about the dying church in Palestine; they care only about supporting Israel."

Bishara: "I was told by a well-meaning Western Christian that, if I am a good Christian, I should just pack up and leave this land in obedience to God because God gave this land to the Jews. If I don't leave, then I deserve the suffering that is coming to me. This is the kind of struggle that we have all the time."

Alex: "We don't want people to hate the Jews. We don't want

Christians to stop supporting Israel in a legitimate way. But to support the settlement movement and the radical Jewish extremists is to support injustice. And that's what many evangelicals are doing right now. They are not discerning, they are not allowing the Holy Spirit to lead them to do the right thing. They are supporting the most radical elements within Jewish society. They don't like the peace movement in Israel. They don't listen to the voice of reason among the Jewish people. They focus on the radicals who want to build settlements and to take the Palestinian land, and these are the ones they are supporting. And that makes us as Palestinian Christians very, very sad. Because we see the ones who are supposed to stand with us and pray for us as totally indifferent to our cause."

Rev. Alex Awad, pastor of East Jerusalem Baptist Church and Dean of Students of Bethlehem Bible College, with his wife, Brenda.

Nihad: "Many people want the coming of Jesus so badly that it doesn't matter if it means doing away with people. God's concern is not the return of Jesus but that people will come to faith in his Son. But there are so many Christians today who believe that they have to bring back Israel so they can convince Jesus to come back. Not to *pray* for it but to *pay* for it.

"When Jesus entered Jerusalem, the Jews cried, 'Save us!' And He did save them, but not the way they wanted Him to. If He would have saved them the way they wanted Him to, Jesus would have to kill the Romans. Jesus did not come to save by killing others. He came to save by giving His own life, by dying for others.

"The heart of God is with His creation, with Jew and Gentile. I think this is often today set aside, and people think that 'My theology is more important than the heart of God. My convictions are more important than treating one another as human beings.' We all do well to study the words of Jesus instead of all the books coming out on end time theology.

"Many come and say they love the believers among the Palestinians. But if we stop there, then we are selfish. Don't support only me and telephone only me and be nice to only me as a child of God. You're going to spend eternity with me. But love the ones who really need our love – the Muslims, the Palestinians and the Jews. They are human beings who need the salvation of the Lord Jesus Christ. They need to see the love of Jesus Christ."

Alex: "Today, the Jewish population of Israel is more than 80 percent non-religious. And most of those are atheists. The 20 percent who would say they are religious [except for Messianic believers] are religious like the sect of the Pharisees during the time of Jesus. If Jesus would come now, they would crucify Him again. So you are talking about a totally secular state."

Listening to our brothers speak, we can hear their struggle between the love and teaching of Jesus and the daily suffering and injustices they endure. I wonder how my faith would fare if tested in this churning cauldron. How easy it is for us in the West to preach about love and righteousness and forgiveness when there is little or no cost involved. Here, however, the cost is great and very, very personal.

Nihad: "One night, about a year ago, a Tanzim gunman (Tanzim is an arm of Yasser Arafat's Fatah party and one of the three main terrorist groups, along with Hamas and Islamic Jihad) ran between my house and the house of my neighbor, Atallah Isawi, a Baptist pastor and teacher here at the college. The gunman fired his rifle at the IDF District Coordinating Officer camp on the hill across from us and then ran away.

"Half an hour later, the electricity went off, and the soldiers began shooting at our homes. They kept shooting for three hours. My wife and I and our children – two daughters, four and seven, and our nine-year-old son – were down on the floor because bullets came in through our house. Our seven-year-old daughter was shivering in my arms. We were praying, and she was so much afraid. After one hour, you think it's going to stop. After two hours, you think it must stop, and you are on the floor, praying, seeking the Lord.

"The children were terrified of all that noise. As each bullet hit the metal door, you could hear it echo through the house. Then they threw 27 concussion bombs. One hit the fence. For several months afterward, my daughters could not sleep alone. You can imagine me and my wife sleeping every night on mattresses on the floor with our three children.

"The next evening, I turned on Middle East Television, and an American Christian program was on. You know, you seek comfort from these programs as a Christian. You might hear a word of encouragement. The host was on a live telephone call to an army captain in an Israeli military camp – the same Israeli soldiers who had been shooting at me and my family and our neighbors for three hours. And the television host was encouraging the officer and telling him that Western Christians are praying for him. At the end of the call, the host said, 'God bless you!'

"I was so upset. This army captain that he was blessing was the one who had been terrifying my children for months. They no longer eat well. All their habits are changed. And then my American brother says to him, 'God bless you.'

"For what? For terrifying my children, children of God? 'May God save you,' yes, I would accept that. 'May God have mercy upon you,' yes. But to bless what the soldiers are doing, no way.

Why will these Christians in the West call a captain who is not even a believer? Why didn't they call believers like me who are being shot at and bless and encourage us?"

From enemies, abuse and injustice are expected. From family, we expect comfort and support. It is painful enough that few in the West have heard their story, but fewer still have even asked for it. And now, with two Westerners eager to listen, our brothers couldn't seem to stop until the whole story was told.

Nihad: "One time there was so much shelling that no one could get out of their home. A lady from our church called on brother Johnny, an elder.

" 'Can you help us?' she begged. 'There is nobody to help us, and we are afraid.'

"So he tried to drive in, get them quickly into his car and get them out. He had done that once before.

"As he approached her house, the Israelis again began shooting. They riddled his car with bullets. The three children in the house were screaming because bullets were coming in everywhere. Her husband was in shock. He called me on the cell phone.

" 'We don't know what to do, pastor, can you come and help us?'

"So I prayed, as I always do before I go out during the curfew, to have a peace about going out. If I have peace about it, I am not afraid. When I got the Lord's peace, I went out, made it to the street behind them and kept contact on the cell phone.

" 'Where are you?' I shouted.

" 'We came out, and they are shooting all around us!'

"As soon as they ran from the house, brother Johnny took the two youngest children in his arms and pushed the husband along. Suna, the man's wife, was behind them.

"Just as I called on the phone, brother Johnny and the whole group came running around the corner. That moment, their house was hit by a rocket and totally destroyed – just minutes after brother Johnny had pulled everyone out. They were all in a state of shock and did not know what to do. The whole family would have been killed.

"Since then, this family has been homeless and still lives here in the House of Hope, an institution for the homeless. Even if they wanted to rebuild, the Israelis would destroy it again, because we fixed it for them once before, and the soldiers destroyed it again. This is one incident. We have had many more."

Alex: "There is also good news in Bethlehem. We are seeing more and more people coming to the Lord. Last December, we had a community meeting with a meal and everything. About 2,000 people came, and more than 400 accepted Jesus as their personal Savior."

Labib said he knows one of the ladies who gave her life to Christ during that outreach. He said that she is a lawyer who used to be one of the leading communist figures in the country.

Alex: "Pastor Nihad can tell you that his church is overflowing, a church that he planted only a few years ago."

Nihad: "The response goes one of two ways as a result of the current conflict. Some reject God totally. 'Where is God?' they say. Others are seeking the truth. With them, there is hope.

"Last Christmas, three groups from our church visited 138 houses of traditional, historical Christians. They came to evangelize and sing and give a gift. Only two houses rejected our visit. Before, half would reject the visit. In Beit Jala and Beit Sahour, 80 percent are traditional Christians. In Bethlehem itself, if you do not count the two suburbs and three refugee camps, 60 percent are traditional Christians. Including the refugee camp populations, the percentage drops to 40 because the camps are almost entirely Muslim.

"There is openness now, which means we need to harvest the remnant.

"The Lord is blessing. We have five evangelical churches in the Bethlehem area. Most are having renewal and expansion. Some are growing slowly. We started in 1999 with 25 people. Now we are, including children, over 150 people, and 80 percent are new believers."

But the continuing violence, especially the current siege, is taking its toll on new and old believers alike. Ron and I experienced just a little of the anxiety as we talked with our brothers, their comments punctuated by rumbling floorboards and rattling glass as tanks continued to thunder past just outside the office window.

Nihad: "Throughout nearly 40 days of siege, many people ask, 'Pastor, what hope do we have here? We have only one life. Why don't we live it somewhere where our children can really have peace?' I look at my children, and the reality is that they are already two months without school, two months trapped in their own house. They have no recreation at all and are terrified. They are growing up with tanks and bullets. What kind of environment am I keeping my children in?

"My wife and I get discouraged because we see all the problems every day. All the time we visit people. They are all tired. They are all depressed. We try in every house to encourage.

" 'We talk a lot about hope,' my wife said recently, 'but why don't we see the reality of it?'

"She is right. I tell our people: 'The Lord takes care of you. He is going to be with you. Keep on being faithful to the Lord. The Lord is my shepherd, I shall not want.' But most of them are still in want of many things.

"One of the ladies, who I consider a strong believer, called me this morning.

" 'Pastor,' she said, 'we are finished. We prayed. We have nothing at all.'

"As their pastor, I don't know what to do. All around me I see the need, the destruction that the Israelis have done, the war. I don't want to blame anybody. Many of my people are thinking of leaving the country. I don't know what to do, except say, 'Lord, it's up to you. If you want to empty this land, it's up to you.'

"I'm not leaving, not because I am an employee of the church;

I am here because there is a call on my life in this area. I am sticking to the call. And many ministers, if it was not for the call of the Lord, would have nothing to stay for.

"I stood last week with my wife and my family, and we prayed. I said, 'Lord, if my children have any damage growing up like this, please, You are the healer of my children. You are the instructor of my children. My children are in Your hands. I trust You. I cannot trust the situation. I cannot trust even escaping to the West to give my children the best I can. Even in the midst of all of this, if I cannot provide the best, at least You can.'

"So at the end, you really have to trust the Lord. That is what gives you the strength and courage to continue.

" 'I am with you,' He says. 'I will not forsake you. My eye is upon you.' "

Alex: "Going to God in prayer is the first source of our support. But also your coming here today is a blessing to us. When people come and ask the questions you have asked, we know that some people care. Yesterday, another person came and brought a donation to the Bible college and asked about us.

"So, in spite of the fact that we said a lot of negative things about the evangelical church in the United States, I want to admit that a growing number of evangelical brothers and sisters love us and send us emails of encouragement and donations to keep us standing on our feet and also donations to help us help the community here in Bethlehem.

"God has really been using us – myself, Bishara, Pastor Nihad and Labib – with The Shepherd's Society (an outreach to the Bethlehem-area community) to minister to many thousands of people through humanitarian aid. And this is made possible by Western evangelical Christians.

"So it's not all bad. We see the negative from some Christians, but we also see the positive. More Christians, more evangelicals are standing in solidarity with us and saying to us, 'Keep on doing the work and God will be with you. We are with you, and we are praying for you.'

"I receive emails from people who say 'We are praying for you daily.' And you can imagine how encouraging this is to us."

Bishara: "We are a light to this community, to the whole community – Muslims and Christians and everybody. So we share God's love. We feed the poor."

On the table in front of us were stacks of yellow cards that entitled the bearer to get donated food for his family.

> "I was hungry," Jesus said, "and you gave me something to eat, I was thirsty and you gave me something to drink, I was a stranger and you invited me in, I needed clothes and you clothed me, I was sick and you looked after me, I was in prison and you came to visit me" (Matthew 25:35-36).

Alex: "Most Palestinians and Christians live together in peace. We coexisted for hundreds of years, eating in the same restaurants, attending the same schools, shopping in the same markets. We live together. But there are factions in Islamic culture that are very separatist.

"We identify with the problems of our people. We see their agony, and we try to help them in time of need.

"In this country, no matter how Christian you are, you cannot separate your theology from your politics. You cannot close your eyes and say you don't want to see the tanks and soldiers. You cannot be in the water and not get wet. But we try to be the light of Christ within this political mess. We try to speak for truth and justice. We try to reflect the reality here to the people in the West. We are in Christ, and we are in politics. And we can't help it.

"I cannot say, 'I don't care what's happening in my country. Let's talk about Jesus.' I cannot do that and be a human being. I consider myself first a Christian, first a child of God. But I am living a real life. I eat food, and I speak politics."

When we left the Bible College, we walked across the parking lot and adjacent field so that Pastor Nihad's car wasn't overloaded for the rocky ride back up the hill. And as we cleared the exposed area and piled into the car, I noticed that I had not given the tanks another thought. It didn't feel like we were risking our lives being out in the open during a deadly military curfew. I now enjoyed the same peace that Nihad had received before he stepped out of his door to fetch us – the same peace he had before going out to rescue one of his families from a tank missile.

There in Bishara's office, Ron and I heard things we had hoped we wouldn't hear. We also experienced God's presence. And our brothers, though deeply wounded and frustrated, were full of the love of Christ, which flowed from them to their traditional Christian and Muslim neighbors.

It was hard to say goodbye to Nihad when we arrived back at the dusty hilltop. As we climbed out of the car, we saw other Palestinians – men and women who lived on Bethlehem's fringes, away from the unblinking military surveillance, who risked their lives trying to get to and from jobs or classes.

Pastor Nihad spoke of his concern for his wife. Every day, for eight and ten hours, she talked on the telephone, listening to problems and fears and concerns, giving comfort and encouragement, until she had nothing more to give. He wanted to get her out for a while, somewhere away from the endless pressures and tension of the West Bank. He wanted to send her and their children where, at least for a week or so, they could breathe easily and rest and maybe be pampered a little.

Notes

[1] Charles M. Sennott, *The Body and the Blood* (Public Affairs, New York, 2001), p. 22.

[2] Matthew Gutman, "What in God's name am I doing here?" (*The Jerusalem Post*, Monday, May 20, 2002).

May 10

But I tell you who hear me: Love your enemies, do good to those who hate you, bless those who curse you, pray for those who mistreat you. . . . Do to others as you would have them do to you. Luke 6:27-28, 31

It is Friday, erev Shabbat, Sabbath eve. Suddenly, the Hyatt Regency is no longer empty. Jews from the settlements have poured in and filled every available room, meaning just about all the rooms but ours.

The men wear kippahs (kee'-pahs), or skullcaps, and most are dressed in dark slacks and white or blue shirts, open at the collar. One wears an automatic pistol holstered on his belt. Army-issue Galil assault rifles are slung over shoulders. Ammunition clips bulge in trouser pockets.

ITEM: A bomb just exploded in Beersheba near the main branch of Bank Hapoalim. It only partially exploded and no one was killed. News reports say 17 people were "lightly injured." Two terrorists were captured.

ITEM: The siege finally lifted at the Church of the Nativity in Bethlehem.

We are going into the Gaza Strip today through the Erez crossing.

ITEM: A 14-year-old Palestinian boy was shot and killed this morning by IDF gunfire when he and two others, aged 10 and 14, approached the border fence and nearby military post at the crossing into Gaza. According to *The Jerusalem Post*, "the soldiers fired warning shots and then towards the suspect persons." The other boys were "treated for leg and chest wounds at the local hospital."

A short while ago, a bus carrying 26 of the Palestinians who had been holed up inside the Church of the Nativity passed through this crossing on their return to Gaza.

*   *   *   *

Ron and I drove to Gaza alone. Labib had called ahead and asked two of the brothers in Gaza City to meet us on the Palestinian side of the crossing.

It was about an hour drive from Jerusalem toward the Mediterranean to the Gaza Strip. The countryside is beautiful with green rolling hills dotted with ancient ruins, churches and monasteries.

Someone once described Israel as being three hours wide, six hours long and six thousand years deep. And I guess that's about as accurate as it gets. To me, it is always The Land, and I am always in awe of it.

We swung onto Rte. 4 which runs all the way through Gaza and down through the Raffa checkpoint into Egypt. At the border, we parked in a vast concrete lot amidst scores of vehicles with "TV" stenciled all over them in duct tape or black electrical tape – an attempt by the world media to alert the warring sides that they are neutral in the hope that they won't shoot. Most of the time it worked; a few times, it didn't. Hence, the sudden appearance of reporters wearing $400 Kevlar-lined flak jackets.

We walked alone toward the Israeli checkpoint, a long, low, stone and glass building that one entered, instead of a dusty, sandbagged bunker that one approached.

Here, in the heat of the intifada, and especially here at the Erez crossing, which had just seen deadly violence and witnessed a hero's welcome for those returning from Bethlehem, Ron and I were perceived as slightly insane. No one in their right mind, barring those carrying a press pass, came to Israel these days. What were we thinking?

The soldiers behind the counter inside the checkpoint compared our passports to what seemed to be a dozen computer lists and finally passed us on.

From there, we had to walk a few hundred yards until we came to the Palestinian checkpoint. Crossing from the Israeli side to the Palestinian side is like walking down the middle of an airport runway. It is a wide, open area where everything is clearly visible from both ends with no opportunities for concealment.

With each step, the hairs on the back of my neck gave me the uncomfortable sensation that we were being watched.

One third of the way from the Palestinian side, a taxi approached and asked if we wanted a ride. We opted to continue walking. A few minutes later, our contacts pulled up. Wa'el Hashwa (Wah-el' Hash'-wah) and Fadi Hilam (Fah'-dee Hil'-lam) are members of Gaza Baptist Church, the only evangelical church in the Gaza Strip. Their pastor is Dr. Hanna Massad (Hah'-nah Mah-sahd'), Gaza's only evangelical pastor. Wa'el and Fadi also work at the Palestinian Bible Society Bookstore, which opened a couple of years ago in Gaza City.

The two men accompanied us through the PA checkpoint, where we signed in. Then we got into their car and drove off.

One point two million people live in the 224 square miles of the Gaza Strip, making it the most heavily populated piece of real estate on earth. Two-thirds of the people are refugees from the 1948 war, the 1967 war or both. Settlements, populated by about 5,000 Israelis (there are 200,000 Israelis in all the settlements of both the West Bank and Gaza[1]) and surrounded by military camps, occupy 40 percent of the land.[2]

The terrain leading up to Gaza City is bleak, much of it in ruins. The city itself is a congested sea of concrete buildings and shops. Though the area was surrounded by Israeli troops poised to plunge in like an armored tidal wave, we saw no IDF soldiers.

An occasional Palestinian soldier lounged in front of a building, seemingly unconcerned that a tank armada might roar down the road at any moment.

The streets were packed with trucks and cars, along with flat carts on steel frames and rubber tires, drawn by horses or donkeys.

About 2,000 of the inhabitants of the Gaza Strip are traditional Christian. The lone evangelical church numbers between 50 and 100 evangelical Palestinian believers. The rest are Muslims.

The Bible Society Bookstore serves the surrounding community. It is a small bookstore by Western standards but well utilized, serving, in addition to a bookstore, as a meeting place, storage facility, offices and classrooms.

We waited downstairs while curious church members filtered in one at a time to see the two brothers from America. A few minutes later, Pastor Hanna arrived, and Wa'el and Fadi accompanied us upstairs where we all sat down at a long library table. The inevitable refreshments were served, which would be followed later by lunch.

A large window was open to the street to let in the spring air. It also let in a steady drone of traffic, punctuated by tooting horns and once or twice by somebody saying something in Arabic over a loudspeaker.

*   *   *   *

Hanna Massad is a thoughtful, soft-spoken man and a native of Gaza.

"My family has always lived here. My mother's family is from Jaffa, close to Tel Aviv. But in 1948, they had to leave everything and come here to Gaza.

"My father's side is from Gaza. We have a document at home that says we own land in Israel, but we lost it in 1948 and are unable to do anything about it. We had hundreds of dunoums (400 dunoums is roughly equivalent to an acre). This is what we heard from our parents growing up and our parents from our grandparents. And this is what our generation will tell the next generation. So when we hear from our parents that we lost something and we are not able to do anything about it, it is just by the grace of God that we are able to forgive.

"This is why many people have hatred and bitterness and hopelessness, and are willing to die, willing to do this and that. It is very sad to see people on both sides kill one another, and it's really not worth it.

Like most Christians in Gaza, Hanna was raised Greek Orthodox.

"When I was 17, however, I got to know the Lord in a personal way. My aunt was born again and went to Gaza Baptist Church. She invited me to go to a youth group. The first time I heard the message of Christ simply and clearly and experienced the love of the people in the meeting, it touched my heart.

"This was fine with my parents, until I asked to be baptized, because it is against the Greek Orthodox tradition. My father refused to allow it. It took about a year of prayer and showing him the love of Christ that I experienced before I received his blessing to be baptized.

Another challenge came in 1987 when the church called Hanna to serve as its pastor.

"It was the first time for the community here to have a local boy to be called to the ministry and to pastor in the same area where he got saved and grew up.

"For me, it was a privilege to be the first local pastor, because usually we have pastors coming from Egypt or Lebanon, because the number of believers here is very small, so there's not much money. But it was difficult for my family and the community to accept."

Between 1987 and 1991, Hanna attended Bethlehem Bible College, after which he went to the United States to study at Fuller Theological Seminary in Pasadena where he earned his Ph.D. in

2000. Since then, he has served Gaza Baptist Church here in the city, while teaching at the Bible College – when he is able to reach it.

About two years ago, in Jordan, he met a young Palestinian believer named Suhad. They fell in love, talked a lot on the phone and spent more and more time together. Finally, Hanna went to meet her family. They were soon engaged, married in the Baptist church in Jordan and returned to live in Gaza.

Several months later, while Hanna was in the States, Suhad went to Amman to visit her parents. Since then, the Israelis have not allowed her to return. Three times, though she has done nothing illegal, they have refused to give her a visa.

"Thousands of people here have the same problem," Hanna explained. "The father is on one side and the wife and children are on the other side. In my case, it is a little easier because we do not have any children. With children, it would be more complicated."

Whether Christian or Muslim, everyone in Gaza shares the same struggle.

"Travel, for example, is nearly impossible. Even in the best of times, Gaza is closed off like a prison, both internally and from Israel proper. The Israeli government has divided it into three sectors, from north to south, and people who live in one sector often are not permitted to travel to another.

"Sometimes the roads open for only a few hours. When things get bad, people often wait for days just to move from one place to another. Many families have been divided. If your parents live in the north and you live in Gaza City 15 miles away, you are unable to visit them. The northern section is Palestinian. Gaza City is in the middle. This causes severe hardships for those trying to shop for food, market goods or reach a hospital.

"The Israelis also control all the water. All of our food comes through one checkpoint, and they can close this checkpoint, which they do when things get bad. There are also shortages of gas, food and many other things. In many places, we don't have good water to drink."

Most of the factories in Gaza have been destroyed by the Israeli army and air force. There is little agriculture. The best land has been confiscated to build Israeli settlements, which they irrigate and plant. Then they sell the produce to the people in Gaza. The people have to buy much of what they need from the Israelis.

"A member of our church is a medical doctor. Most of his land has been confiscated by the Israeli soldiers. They did that only because his land is close to one of the settlements. Sometimes people hide behind trees and shoot at the settlements. So the soldiers confiscate the whole area. I have friends whose homes have been destroyed, their land destroyed – all because they happen to be close to the settlements, and the settlers want a buffer zone so they can see everything. While Israel does have legitimate security concerns, it is very sad and very hurtful for us. This is the life we live."

A stronghold of Hamas, the Gaza Strip has been under siege for nearly three years.

"The only exit we have is Raffa (opening into Egypt) for virtually all the people in Gaza. I used to teach at Bethlehem Bible College, but I am no longer able to go since September two years ago. Because of the siege, you are not able to go to the West Bank or to Jerusalem or to Israel. Because people cannot move, few can work. Unemployment is more than 75 percent, according to a spokesman for the United Nations. Many cannot provide food for their families."

Reaching the West Bank, a 40-minute drive, generally takes about four days, because Palestinians have to travel the length of the Gaza Strip, across guarded roads leading to some of the 19 Israeli settlements, through the Raffa checkpoint in the south, into Egypt, across Egypt to Jordan, up through Jordan to the Allenby Bridge, and across the Allenby Bridge over the Jordan River into Jericho.

The return trip can take weeks, depending on how long travelers are forced to wait at the Raffa checkpoint, sometimes sleeping for days in the open.

*   *   *   *

While the handful of Palestinian Christian believers share the same sufferings and frustrations as their Muslim neighbors, they also take every opportunity to share blessings with them.

"Many of us in this congregation desire to share the gospel, share the love of Christ, especially in these difficult days. Through friends of the church, we have been able to help hundreds of families in the city and in the refugee camps over the past two years with food and other necessities.

"When you help a Muslim father who is not able to provide for his children, he will never forget it. But our hearts are really to not just give them a fish but to teach them to fish. So we plan to teach them how to start small businesses so they can take care of their families. This builds good relationships, and through that, we share the love of Christ.

"When things get really bad, we see more openness among the people. They don't know where to go or what to do, so they come to us to ask questions. Some come to the meetings. More are willing to listen, and we see more hunger for the truth and for the gospel."

An increasing desire among Muslims to hear the gospel, however, does not mean that it is safe to share it.

"If we start to do evangelism and they find out, it can put our lives in jeopardy. Once my life was threatened by someone whose sister started to come to the meeting. PA secret police come here to the bookstore and also to the church from time to time to see who is coming.

"On one hand, the Palestinians are not very much against evangelism. The Palestinian Authority is secular and doesn't care much whether we evangelize or if Muslims accept Christ. But they are afraid of sedition. They are afraid that the militant Muslims will find out and come to attack us. A number of times, on the other side of town, the extremists burned a Christian library because they knew that people would come and hear the gospel in that library."

The always-present danger, however, does not stop Hanna and his church from embracing Muslim believers.

"Muslims grow up being taught that Christians are people of blasphemy, that the Bible has been corrupted, Jesus was not crucified or raised from the dead, and Christians believe in three gods. These are very big obstacles that prevent Muslims from coming to know Christ."

After we arrived in Israel, we had heard the account of a Muslim believer I'll call Abdullah. His parents are Palestinian, but his family moved around a lot, and he was born and raised in Mecca, Saudi Arabia, where he grew up to become an extremely fundamentalist Muslim. His fervor even caused his entire family to become zealous for Islam.

Abdullah sincerely wanted to know God and strictly followed the letter of the Koran. He made several pilgrimages to Mecca.

When his family moved to another Saudi city, he met evangelical Palestinian believers for the first time.

At first, he was like Saul. He caused a lot of trouble for the believers, convinced that his persecution of Christians was service to God. But he was moved by the love he saw the believers had for one another. When one lost something, all of them looked for it. When one was happy, all were happy.

Abdullah began asking questions. But like the believers in the book of Acts, they were afraid to say anything to him. Saudi Arabia is consistently recognized by organizations like Open Doors with Brother Andrew as the least religiously tolerant country in the world. So, instead of answering his questions, they gave him a book about Jesus.

As he read it, Abdullah realized that Jesus is the Son of God. And from that time on, he continued going to the mosque and praying, but now he prayed in the name of Jesus. He even changed the words of the Arabic prayers so that they lined up with the Bible.

When his family returned to Palestine, the first thing he did was find a copy of the Bible, which is contraband in Saudi Arabia. The second thing he did was to locate other believers and a church, which he attended in secret, arriving just after the service started, sitting in the back and leaving just before it ended.

One day, his parents discovered his Bible and burned it. And in accordance with Islamic law, his father set out to kill him. His father was known as an excellent marksman and had many guns in the house.

One night, as Abdullah slept, his father crept into his bedroom, pointed a gun an inch away from his head and fired. The bullet missed. The Lord had miraculously protected him.

Another time, as Abdullah walked in his orchard, his father again tried to shoot him. Again and missed. Abdullah was kicked out of the house, and for the next year and a half, he lived alone.

Today, Abdullah and his family are reconciled, and he is sharing the truth with other Muslims.

In John 12:32, Jesus said, "I, when I am lifted up from the earth, will draw all men to myself." He spoke of the death that He would die. But these words also describe what is happening today in the Gaza Strip, as the lives of a few score Christians lift up Jesus in the midst of a despairing Muslim community.

"More people and families are open to hear about the gospel, especially here at the Bible Society Bookstore. More and more students are coming and asking questions about Christ. Sometimes we get 10 men a day, 300 a month asking questions.

"We have even been asked by officials of several ministries of the Palestinian Authority to come and teach leadership courses to their employees. We teach one group here at the bookstore and another in the government building — about 30 students in all, many of whom are doctors and engineers in very high positions and nearly all from the refugee camps. We use John Maxwell's leadership materials. My wife and I translated much of them into Arabic."

Pastor Hanna's vision, however, extends beyond reaching the community with the gospel to seeing peace and unity between Arab and Jewish believers.

"I was looking at the Abrahamic covenant as a foundation to see how the descendants of Ishmael and Isaac, beginning with Palestinian Christian believers and Jewish believers, can be reconciled through Christ. The current political situation doesn't allow us to put this into practice. Years ago, when things were better, we worshiped with our Jewish brothers and sisters. That was a miracle by itself.

"I remember one meeting when a Palestinian brother prayed, 'God give me enough love to be willing to die for my Jewish brother.' And a Jewish believer prayed for the love to give his life for his Arab brother. This is a very moving experience to see how God can work in our hearts to bring us closer to Him and closer to our brothers.

"One man in our congregation lost his blood brother and struggled a lot inside with hatred and bitterness. Little by little, as he experienced the love of God, he was able to overcome the hatred. Forgiveness and how to forgive are things I must continually teach to my people."

Living in this indescribably oppressive corner of the world and dealing constantly with new offenses and the mandate to forgive, these believers need a great deal of support – first from the Lord, but also from their brothers and sisters in the West.

"Even though many times we feel isolated and lonely living under siege in this big prison, we know that we belong to a bigger family, the family of God. We belong to one body, the body of Christ. It is a big encouragement to see you coming and Ron coming, to know that we are working together in the kingdom of God.

"Listening to our story and praying for us and getting a better understanding of who we are is a very big encouragement for us – just to know that you know and understand. Many people in

America don't really know that there are Christians here.

"One day, when I was in the States, I was dressed very nicely for a meeting, and a friend asked why. I told him, jokingly, that I just didn't want people to think that I came all the way from Gaza to Fuller riding a donkey. A lot of people were surprised when they learned that I was from the Gaza Strip. They didn't think there were Christian believers in Palestine. And usually their first thought is that you are from a Muslim background.

"Actually, Christianity here in Palestine goes back all the way to Acts 2, which mentions Arabs among the crowds at Pentecost. The sad thing is that tradition took over many of the early churches. Even though the message of the gospel started in Jerusalem and spread, when the tradition took over, the people no longer experienced a personal relationship with the Lord. Now, however, the message is returning to us. And we hope and pray that the message will again leave here, from Palestine, to other Arab countries around the world."

In America, we are told only part of the story of the conflicts in the Middle East. We are led to believe that Arabs and Jews have been at war with one another since Isaac and Ishmael and will continue to hate one another until Jesus returns. But this is far from the truth.

Hanna explained, "Arabs and Jews lived side by side together in peace for many years. The Arabs don't blame the Jews for the oppression and injustices. They blame secular Zionism and oppose the secular Zionist nationalists who came with a plan to pull the land out from under their feet. They felt threatened, and the conflict started.

"Many Western Christians know that Israel became a state in 1948, but few know that when it did, more than 700,000 Palestinians became refugees and 50,000 of those were Christians – Catholic and Greek Orthodox. These people became refugees, scattered around the world. That's when the problem of Palestinian refugees began.

"It is difficult as Palestinian Christian believers to watch our

Western brothers and sisters support secular Israel 100 percent, sometimes unconditionally. We read in the papers and see on television that 70 million evangelical Christians in America fully support Israel. So my Muslim friends say, 'Oh, you are a Christian.' And we appear in their eyes like secular Zionists (see Appendix II) or collaborators or traitors.

"This places a large stumbling block in the path of their salvation, and makes it very difficult for us to reach them. Little by little, however, they learn who we are and that we are not secular Zionists, that our focus is on the Lord, not on the Land.

"We understand that one responsibility of a Christian is to speak out against injustice. We see this in Amos and Isaiah:

> Is not this the kind of fasting I have chosen: to loose the chains of injustice and untie the cords of the yoke, to set the oppressed free and break every yoke? Is it not to share your food with the hungry and to provide the poor wanderer with shelter—when you see the naked, to clothe him, and not to turn away from your own flesh and blood? Then your light will break forth like the dawn, and your healing will quickly appear (Isaiah 58:6-8).

"When something is wrong, it is wrong. Christianity is not about politics. It is about Jesus Christ.

"We have our moments asking what we are doing here. My wife is in Amman, I am not able to move freely and life is very difficult. We live under siege. But God has given us hope and helped us to keep going. I stay because God gave me a heart for my people and for Gaza and called me to minister here.

"If we just keep focusing on the problems, we will fall into despair like Elijah when he ran from Jezebel. But his love which is in our hearts keeps us moving and hoping and able to minister to the people around us."

As we talked, we quickly recognized Wa'el and Fadi as Hanna's right-hand men. Serious, helpful Wa'el and Fadi-of-the-Ready-Laugh. These two young men also are the backbone of the bookstore ministry – evangelistic to the core. They are excited about the new openness to the gospel among their Muslim neighbors and constantly look for creative ways to initiate and build more relationships.

Ron Brackin, Dr. Hanna Massad, and Wa'el Hashwa at Gaza Baptist Church

"Many people come here and ask about Jesus Christ and the gospel," Wa'el explained. "Sometimes, they ask what I believe and whether the Bible is true or false. We answer their questions. We give Bibles and New Testaments to those who ask for them. We also offer inexpensive French and English courses. Many university students study languages with us. We also teach leadership courses. Many leaders from the PA come here for those courses. Some of them, after discussions, have accepted Jesus Christ as Savior.

"Also we have a relationship with the various government agencies, and we participate in the Palestinian and international book fairs."

Wa'el was born and raised in Gaza. He is an only child, a rarity in a region where, according to a recent census, the average Palestinian woman bears 7.5 children. [3] Like most of the believers, Wa'el's parents are Greek Orthodox. When he accepted Christ in 1987 at 14, his parents said it was okay, having concluded that all churches are alike.

Wa'el studied business administration at Al Quds Open University, working part time for the Palestine Trade Union Federation. After graduation, he attended seminary in Egypt for two years, then returned to Gaza. He currently works with the Bible Society.

Wa'el was recently engaged to Patricia Ghubar. The couple had to travel to Jordan for their engagement (in the Middle East, an engagement celebration is a major family affair) because Wa'el cannot go to Bethlehem, where Patricia lives, and she cannot come to Gaza. Since the Bethlehem siege began, they can only talk to one another on the cell phone. So Wa'el and Patricia call each other many times a day, and Wa'el immerses himself in his ministry.

"I see God's hand working in the church here in Gaza. Several years ago, we had no permanent pastor. Pastor Hanna was in the U.S., completing his education. Few believers came to church, and there was no growth. In 1999, the Bible Society Bookstore opened, and Hanna came to pastor us. Then many people started to accept Christ and come to church, and they are growing."

Wa'el's eyes light up even more as he tells us about the children's ministries.

"It's very nice to work with children. We have an Olive Club children's ministry to 45 children, all from outside the church. Fadi and I, along with an American volunteer with a Palestinian background and a few other volunteers, taught the children some English and stories about God. After that we had a big party for 300 children where we taught songs about the peace of God. We are planning four more activities for the children in the refugee camps. Perhaps this summer."

But the church is small and could use some outside help.

"We need Western Christian believers to come with us to see what we are doing. We need one or two volunteers to teach English."

"We also need volunteers who are gifted in the area of music in the church and also in our outreach ministries," Hanna added. "A lot of the work for the children can be done through music. Our workers want very much to learn piano and guitar; and we need volunteers to teach drama."

Until now, Fadi has sat, listened, grinned and done supreme justice to the pita bread and falafel. You can't help being drawn by his grin (he rarely just smiles) and his unquenchable enthusiasm.

Fadi is 25, a native of Gaza. His father died, and he has two brothers, neither of whom is a believer. His mother is a believer but not quite ready to switch to Gaza Baptist Church.

"She is happy to hear about the gospel and to read the Bible and go to church and to sing. She likes that," Fadi explained. "She knows the Lord, but she still goes to the Greek Orthodox Church."

Fadi has been a believer for seven years. A month ago, he became engaged to a young woman in Gaza who is currently studying English Literature at university.

Even though Fadi and his fiancé live in the same town, engagement and marriage are difficult for evangelical Palestinians.

"Fadi is only the second local to be engaged in an evangelical church in Gaza," Hanna explained. "This is very new for the Christian culture. It is a big challenge, because everyone else gets engaged and married in the traditional churches.

"To be a Palestinian Christian means to be Greek Orthodox or

Catholic. It's not just the faith; it's the culture. So if you become evangelical, you cut yourself off from the community. It's like the blind boy in John 9. When he believed, he risked being excommunicated. The challenge we face when we become evangelical is how we can now relate to the community. Many of our traditional Christian neighbors look down on us. Some think what we did is horrible.

"So when Fadi said he wanted to be engaged in the evangelical way, there was a lot of resistance from his family, a lot of attacking and challenging. But he was brave to stand for what he believes, and Wa'el the same."

"It's a new thing in Gaza," Fadi said. "In the evangelical engagement celebration, we present the gospel, which is the first time most of the family members ever heard the message of Jesus Christ clearly. The engagement ceremony is very brief in the traditional church. In ours, there is the gospel and music and worship and a party – much longer. It's a good way to share the gospel with Christians."

Sharing the gospel – with Christians of limited understanding and with others outside the church altogether – is the power that drives Fadi Hilam.

"God has called me to evangelism. I like to speak with people, to open doors to people, to speak about Jesus. I used to be afraid to speak to people, but God has now given me a great burden and boldness. I had a dream where I saw a Bible as a bridge and the Holy Spirit coming to the people of Gaza, and many coming from all directions and crying to accept Jesus."

"We have an idea in mind to have house churches," said Hanna. "Fadi is leading a home group of young people. We hope to have more groups spread out in different areas. We want to include all people, including Muslim believers.

"On Sunday mornings at the church, we usually have about 50 people and 50 more on Sunday evening. So if there are five Muslim believers in each meeting, it is not a problem. But the community of believers is very small. Everyone knows everyone and everything about everyone. So a strange face stands out, and if there are very many strange faces, people get nervous.

"The challenge as a pastor is to love the whole community, traditional Christians on one hand and also the Muslims. But the Christians do not accept the Muslims, so how do you balance the two? You don't want to win one group and lose the other.

"Fadi and Wa'el and the Bible Society reach to those who have not been touch with the Gospel. In the past, about 300 students a month would come from the universities to ask questions – fewer now during the current political situation. So how do you have separate ministry for these new believers? Do you disciple them one on one or bring them together in homes in small groups? This is the challenge."

"This morning a man came in from a place along the border where there are no Christians, no Bibles, nothing," said Fadi. "He accepted Jesus Christ by correspondence, and he asked me to come to his village, because many there want to know Jesus, want to hear about Jesus and to see the *Jesus Film*. God put that in him. I see the hunger, but the Israelis have closed the road. I cannot go, and we need much prayer to open the way."

"People here in Gaza see how we relate to one another," Hanna said, "with love and respect. And many are saying, 'Oh, we like that. We want to be part of this kind of relationship.' The love of Christ in His people touches their hearts."

It touched our hearts, too. And the nagging question remained. Could I love as they do under the same circumstances. I tried to imagine being separated from my wife, Lisa, for eight months with no hope of the government letting her return home. Would I become bitter and cynical? Would I remain here and continue to shepherd a tiny flock of believers under Israeli military occupation in the midst of more than a million Muslims? Or would I join my wife and start our lives over in America or Europe?

As always, it was difficult to leave our new friends. But we were scheduled to rendezvous with Labib and drive to the

Palestinian Bible Society offices near the Garden Tomb in East Jerusalem.

*   *   *   *

Arab East Jerusalem is dramatically different from the Jewish side of the city. It's close and tangled. Dingy and in disrepair. Absent is the freshly swept, manicured feel of West Jerusalem.

As at the Gaza bookstore, the ground floor walls of the Bible Society were lined with shelves of Bibles, New Testaments, and other Arabic-language Christian literature. Several offices were in the back and an iron staircase wound in a narrow spiral to the upper floor.

Prominently displayed on the wall behind Labib's desk is a large color photograph of King Hussein bin Talal, deeply revered by his people as the Father of modern Jordan. Labib, a handsome young Jordanian who resembles the king in his youth, affectionately shared several stories about this unusual monarch.

Then with even more affection and passion, Labib told us about the origins of the Bible Society's newest ministry to Palestinian children.

"We were coming back from a Bible Society conference at the beginning of the current intifada. A number of children already had been killed in the Israeli retaliation. Shortly after we arrived, the Israeli army invaded Bethlehem for the first time. There was heavy shelling and shooting. You heard some stories from Pastor Nihad yesterday.

"So we wondered what we could do for the people here. Our team came together to pray and share ideas. Children were our main concern. Children have been so terribly traumatized, so scared. They are the real victims of the situation. And our hearts were broken to see this happening. What would Jesus do? Every day, the news was filled with more photos of pain and suffering. Our choice was to ignore it and get on with business, succumb to hate and bitterness and revenge – or stand up and act.

"So we asked God for grace and wisdom to put together a program. It was around Christmas, and Bethlehem was completely closed. One of my colleagues who is responsible for our work in Bethlehem, said, 'Palestinian children cannot come to Bethlehem, so why can't we take Bethlehem to them?'

"The program was simply to let the children have fun with Jesus – to laugh, to play, to have some competition sports and games, to have the joy of unwrapping some gifts, to hear stories about Jesus, to know that Jesus still loves them; and it was amazing how well it was received.

"Once, in a school in the Bethlehem area, one of the teachers named Samar was looking at 200 kids joyfully opening Christmas gifts, and she just broke out in tears.

" 'I've never seen my kids so happy,' she said. 'Last night, they were surrounded by the shooting and shelling, and now they are completely in another world, really having fun with Jesus, knowing that Jesus still loves them.'

"Over time, the ministry extended, as more and more schools and communities invited us in. Love knows no discrimination. Several Muslim schools and communities actually invited us.

"Last week in Beir Zeit (Beer Zite'), there were 250 Muslim kids. They watched puppet shows about Bible stories, all of which say that God is our Father and he cares for us. The puppets speak of forgiveness, love, peace, the fruit of the Spirit; and we taught the kids songs.

"One Muslim village actually invited us to conduct a summer camp. So we had a two-week summer camp in that village with all the children singing, 'Glory, glory, hallelujah!' They had never sung that. They sang, 'Father Abraham has many sons. I am one of them, and so are you. So let's just praise the Lord!' Muslim kids! Singing, 'This is the day that the Lord has made' in Arabic.

"Some people in the village went to the sheik, the Muslim mayor, complaining, 'What are these songs about *glory* and *hallelujah*?' And he told them, 'No problem, they're just praising God.

Hallelujah means *Praise the Lord!* That's fine.'

"Every day, all these children see is persecution – tanks, shooting, blockades, siege, imprisoning them in their own villages and houses. All they hear is talk of revenge and bitterness and killing and provocation and incitement and calls for jihad. The songs they sing are about martyrdom. All they are taught all their lives is about conflict.

"So when they sing about peace, you just see the joy in their faces. Enjoying it, loving it, laughing. I believe by doing this we are really counteracting evil by the goodness of Jesus. This is my formula.

"Certainly, I want to expose the crimes of Israel to the whole world. Yes, I want to expose the crimes of the Palestinian terrorists to the whole world. I can say this must be punished and that must be punished. Justice is justice, and justice always should be done. But instead, I have decided to give the fire for justice to God and take from His hands the fire of mercy, and take it to the people.

"It's painful. Many times your heart is just boiling. We listened in Bethlehem to the stories about the parents who had to bury their daughter in their backyard garden because the army would not let them go to the nearby hospital to save her. It is tough. If it was my daughter, I don't know if I would be speaking softly.

"But if I'm not a direct victim, I want to go to the direct victims, and instead of fueling their anger and hatred and their understandable feelings for revenge, I want to tell them that somebody cares.

"So we go to the children. And you know, when parents and the community see what is happening with their children, it affects them a lot.

"We were invited by a Muslim society in Gaza that had about 400 kids. And before they turned the program over to us, they did some Koran reading. And they chanted 'We are millions of martyrs marching on towards Jerusalem.' This is becoming like a national anthem.

"I don't want this to be the national anthem of the Palestinian people. I reject it. I want to vote for life, not for death. The word *liberation* carries within it life, not death.

"Our team took over after their part was finished. Before we began, it felt like an evil spirit just was hovering over everything. We immediately started with the story that Jesus told about the king who forgave his servant and how the servant did not forgive his servant and so on. So we addressed the necessity to forgive as a way of counteracting the spirit of hatred with the Spirit of Jesus, not with the spirit of anti-Islam.

"Then we taught them to sing a song of peace. It's a well-known song. We sing it in our churches: '*Salam salam li sha'b el rab fi kulli makan* (Peace, peace to God's people everywhere!). Then our team leader started to sing the names of Palestinian cities in the song, singing, 'Peace, peace to Nablus, to the people of God in Nablus and Jenin' and so on. 'Peace, peace to the people of God in Gaza and Rafah.' And all 400 kids sang that song with the loudest voice until the program concluded.

"It started with martyrdom. It ended with singing for peace. And all the kids were running in the tiny streets of the refugee camp, hundreds of voices, singing 'Peace, peace to God's people wherever they are!' This was a breakthrough. This was a victory!"

Labib went on to explain how God is continuing to bless their efforts to turn the next generation away from hatred, violence and revenge.

"Near Bir Zeit, there are two other Muslim villages who welcomed us with that same program. Near Nablus, there are five. Two or three weeks ago, the Union of Kindergartens in the Governorate of Salfit, an area of 60,000 people in the Palestinian territories, brought 300 kids with their teachers from more than 20 kindergartens and attended a half-day program of songs, magic, games, promoting Bible ethics, stories Jesus told, gifts for the kids — a day of celebration and joy. No more tanks. No more soldiers. No more bombs. No more martyrdom. No more politics. Just Jesus and children and joy.

"Our main task is to lead the Palestinian people into a personal encounter with Jesus Christ through reading the Bible and learning its relevance for their lives. As much as possible, we use every avenue to make the Word of God available to the Palestinian people.

"In order to do that, we do not run campaigns. By that I mean that we do not do hit-and-run crusades, in and out. Once in, we are in. And we stay, because we do not see ourselves as an organization outside the society and just making deliveries. In our hearts, we are part of the Palestinian people. We belong here. We are carrying Christ to our own people.

"So this is the foundation of our ministry. Nor do we see Islam as a target to attack or to expose or anything of that sort. We look at Muslims as our beloved people, as family, and we want them to get the chance to read the Bible and to know about Christ and God's love for them.

"We maintain a positive, active presence within the Palestinian society. That's why we started by establishing Bible Centers in the most populated areas such as the Gaza Strip. We have already begun to establish a new center in Nablus in the northern portion of the West Bank, an area of some 150,000 people, including 600 Christians and a few believers. There is one Anglican Church there, two Catholic and one Orthodox. As yet, there is no evangelical congregation.

"We also have a Student Center – a ministry directed to the university students – in Bir Zeit, where the main Palestinian university is located. Most of the Palestinian leadership have either studied or taught there.

"Most recently, we partnered with other ministries to launch an outreach through internet chat rooms in which specially trained volunteers go into chat rooms, especially Palestinian chat rooms, to bring in the biblical perspective. The goal of this internet ministry is to start special Bible chat rooms for every Palestinian university.

"As you see, we are trying to make the Palestinian Bible Society as proactive as possible. We do not wait for people to come to our center. We build relationships with the community around us.

Over the years, we have built strong relationships within the Palestinian Ministry of Education, the Ministry of Culture and with universities and public libraries.

"This intifada has already continued much longer than anyone expected, and it's becoming very heavy on people. Many, many casualties, and the people are really suffering. Recently, I was reading the Bible and came across Isaiah 40:1-5 that says;

> Comfort, comfort my people, says your God. Speak tenderly to Jerusalem, and proclaim to her that her hard service has been completed, that her sin has been paid for, that she has received from the Lord's hand double for all her sins. A voice of one calling: 'In the desert prepare the way for the Lord; make straight in the wilderness a highway for our God. Every valley shall be raised up, every mountain and hill made low; the rough **ground** shall become level, the rugged places a plain. And the glory of the Lord will be revealed, and all mankind together will see it. For the mouth of the Lord has spoken.

"Immediately after the command to bring comfort, the prophet talks about the coming of Jesus, the coming of Jesus. Prepare the way for the Lord. And I really hope that what we are doing is that we are preparing the way for the Lord to come into the lives of many Palestinians.

"This is the way I want to comfort my people. This is the call. It's not a political call. It's not an anti-Israel or anti-Muslim call, God forbid! It's simply the heart of God. God is crying."

Just then, we were informed that a special visitor had arrived.

*   *   *   *

Shehade Shahin (Sheh-hahd' Shah-heen'), known affectionately as Abu Sleiman (Ah-boo' Slee'-mahn), which means Father of
Sleiman, climbed the spiral staircase, entered Labib's office and sat
down. He moved easily like a man in his sixties, not at all as you
would expect of a man who was one hundred ten years old.

Understandably, we hoped to hear a firsthand, living account
of history. What we got was much more than we had expected.

*Abu Sleiman is 110 years
old, remembers much,
but dwells only on Jesus.*

"I was born in 1892 in Nablus during the occupation of the
Ottoman Turks under the reign of Sultan Abdul Hamid," Abu
Sleiman told us. "We don't have a family tree, but I know that my
father, my grandfather, my great grandfather all lived here. We
have been living here always. There are some Shahins that are
Muslims, so it seems that at some point in the past a section of our
family was converted to Islam, but the Shahin has always been a
Christian family in Palestine.

"During the Turkish occupation, it was very bad. Most of the
Palestinians were very poor with no education. No schools. Most
people were in farming.

"My father worked in textiles, making clothes. We had some orchards, olive trees and so on. I worked a lot because I didn't have an education. I worked in agriculture, just a day worker; I worked in hotels, in kitchens.

"When I was maybe 16 or 17, I was taken to serve in the Turkish army. A Turkish officer came to get us and brought some loaves of bread and started throwing it to us like dogs. That showed me that army life was going to be very bad for us. So I ran away. I hid in my house for four years until the Turks were defeated and the British came at the end of World War I.

"I was lost then. I am very sorry that I was far from the Lord for so many years. I accepted him when I was 45 or 50.

"One of my children used to go to the Baptist bookstore in Jerusalem, and this son of mine received Christ because there was a church next to the bookstore. So I started going with my son to that church. When I saw his life change because of Christ, I started going to evangelical churches.

"I thank the Lord all my children are believers. One of my sons is a pastor in Bethlehem. One is a pastor with Trans World Radio. One is a doctor in the States. One is a businessman, and another is in the computer business. Five boys and four girls. Many grandchildren. My daughter's son is married and has children. Four generations."

Abu Sleiman is twice a widower. His third wife is 68. She has diabetes, which necessitated the amputation of one of her feet.

When we asked about his health, Abu Sleiman said, "This is from the Lord. I have no diabetes, no high blood pressure, no sicknesses at all. My only problem now is I have some pain in my knees. Praise the Lord. It's all right. With this age, it's very good. I depend on the Lord, like in Proverbs 3:1-2:

> My son, do not forget my teaching, but keep my commands in your heart, for they will prolong your life many years and bring you prosperity.

"I sleep well, walk well. Everything is good. Praise the Lord!"

We encouraged him to describe to us what it was like for him as a Palestinian Christian living under so many different occupations over more than a century. But our venerable brother would talk only about the Lord.

"Why do you try to break my head?" he asked gently. "If I'm a believer, it makes no difference to me who is in power. I don't care. I never got myself involved in politics. I read newspapers. I got to know what's happening around. And I refuse to get into politics. Politics is a headache. Praise the Lord, I am a believer. That's enough. Whether we live or die, we are the Lord's.

"The most important thing in my life is my relationship with the Lord and my relationship with anyone I meet, whenever the Lord would enable me to tell them about Christ. This is my world and this is what I care about.

"The issue in Palestine is not about difficulty. It is about love. Love is so scarce. People pray but only worship with their words. Not like James says, 'Faith without works is dead.'

"Within the family of believers, there is no love. People don't listen to each other. They are Christians in name only. I have three neighbors in the same building who are Christian families. But they never think, 'Let's go to Abu Sleiman and let's read the Bible or pray together.' It is as if I speak English and they speak Turkish.

"The Christians of the nations, are they working with the Lord? They are not. If Christians were working really according to the Bible, you would find more Muslims and Jews coming to faith in Christ. People are attracted to what is good, so if they see that Christ is good in our lives, they will come to Christ."

With the rare opportunity to speak with a 110-year-old man who has spent most of his life completely devoted to Jesus, I wanted to know what his life message would be to the world.

"The most important thing I would say to people is to live the life of faith and doing the works of faith. The second thing I would say is, you have your Bible. Follow the Bible."

There was nothing more any of us could add after that. So we all bowed our heads and spoke together with God.

Notes

[1] Dan Perry, Associated Press, "35 years later, Six Day War is still being fought" (*The Dallas Morning News*, Sunday, June 9, 2002), p.25A.

[2] Charles M. Sennott, *The Body and the Blood* (Public Affairs, New York, 2001), p. 116.

[3] Matthew Gutman, "What in God's name am I doing here?" (*The Jerusalem Post*, Monday, May 20, 2002).

May 11

He has showed you, O man, what is
good. And what does the Lord require of
you? To act justly and to love mercy and to
walk humbly with your God. Micah 6:8

ITEM: IDF forces are still building up along the Gaza Strip.
We may have made it in and out just in time.

ITEM: In Bethlehem, Roman Catholics, Greek Orthodox and
Armenian Orthodox clergy are busy cleaning up the Church of the
Nativity. *The Jerusalem Post*, at the end of the siege yesterday,
described the mess: "the basilica reeked of urine. The stone floor
was covered with dirty blankets and mattresses, lighters, sun-
glasses, a toothpaste tube, a bottle of aftershave, plastic bags, ciga-
rette butts, a comb, and large cooking pots. A stove and gas
canisters for cooking stood to one side of the central aisle.
Leftover food covered an altar in the Armenian section." Damages
included several broken windows and fire-gutted rooms. And "a
statue of the Virgin Mary in the courtyard took a bullet in the
shoulder."

*　　*　　*　　*

We finished breakfast, and Labib called Jack Sara (Sah'-rah),
pastor of the Jerusalem Alliance Church in the Muslim Quarter of
the Old City, who agreed to meet with us at our hotel.

Jack is 28 years old. I mention this first because I found it amazing and still do.   The longer we talked, the more I was impressed by the wisdom and character God had developed in him in so few years.

Jack Sara, the first ordained pastor of the Jerusalem Alliance Church in the Old City's Muslim Quarter.

It also seemed strange to be talking to a Palestinian named "Jack." But he explained that Jack is really a very common name here, especially in the traditional Christian community; his name is actually Jacub, after his grandfather.

Jack was born and raised in the Old City. He is from a traditional Catholic family and came to know the Lord in 1991. Prior to that time, he was a long way from Jesus Christ.

"I came from a hard political background," Jack explained. "Actually, I didn't want to be involved in politics. I was just walking one of the streets in the Old City one day during the first intifada while a demonstration was going on, and a soldier came over to me, picked me up and took me to the police station. They beat me up there, and I really didn't do anything. I was just 15 years old, and I didn't want anything to do with it.

"Then exactly the same thing happened again. That's when I decided that the next time I went to prison it would be for something I did. So I became involved with a communist group that was active in the city, young people who were zealous to do something to change the situation.

"Between 1988 and 1991, I was in prison seven times, usually for only a few weeks. The last time, when I was 17, I served three months. I realized then that I didn't want to continue like this. I wanted to do something serious that really could change things in the lives of my people. So I thought I would become a counselor or a social worker, something to identify with my people on a more intellectual level. I came out of prison and finished high school.

"Over the next eight months, I searched for meaning. I quit all my political associations.

"In July, 1991, my family moved to another house in the Old City, next door to a local pastor named Hanna Katanashu (Kah-ta-nah'-shoo). He was a different kind of guy. He wasn't Catholic like the rest of us in the neighborhood. He had different kinds of views of Christians, and I wanted to talk to him.

"On August 10, I saw him passing by with Labib and said, 'Hanna, I want to talk with you. Can I come and just discuss things with you? I have a few questions.'

"As he and Labib presented the gospel to me, I forgot all my questions and accepted the Lord. And immediately, the Holy Spirit began working in my life.

"I enrolled in the Bethlehem Bible College, studied Christian Education, and lead worship on the keyboard. At the end of my third year, the Lord's call on my life to serve as a pastor was strong."

So Jack left Jerusalem and went to the Philippines to earn his Master of Divinity degree at the Alliance Biblical Seminary in Manila. In 1999, after his return, he was ordained, married a beautiful young believer named Madleine, and shortly thereafter was installed as senior pastor.

"For half a century, the Jerusalem Alliance Church had no permanent pastor. I was the first one. For a while, the church was led by a committee of two men and two women (one of the women was Linda Kasheshian, whom we had met in Ramallah), which underlines the important role that women play in our church ministries. After that, Labib pastored as a lay leader for four years."

To Westerners, Jack's church is unique for several reasons. For one thing, most of us would naturally expect to find a Christian church in the Christian Quarter rather than in the heart of the Muslim Quarter. For another, few of us can imagine being part of a Sunday morning service in which Jesus is praised and worshiped in Arabic. In addition, this congregation is made up of an unusually large number of Muslim believers – one out of ten church members comes from an Islamic background.

"Ten years ago, it wasn't easy for a Muslim to be part of a church. He was not accepted as much as he is now, and he is still not welcome in some evangelical churches. These churches have had bad experiences. They have been hurt by Muslims who say 'We believe in Jesus,' but turned out to be infiltrators or spies. Many pretended to be believers just for the advantages – marrying a girl, money, etc. The Christian lifestyle is different from the Muslim lifestyle.

"In the West Bank and Gaza, it is dangerous for churches to be known as evangelizing Muslims. If a Muslim becomes an *infidel*, his family is allowed to kill him to reduce the shame. And who would know? The Israeli police ignore the everyday problems of the Palestinian people – alcoholism, violence, etc. – things they would not tolerate in West Jerusalem. One of the Muslim believers I have been discipling said, 'My cousins came to me, put a gun to my head and tried to kill me.' Fortunately, he was a really tough guy and fought his way out."

Jack encourages Muslim believers to be part of his church because he is convinced that they are vital to church growth. He sees the influx of new believers coming much more from Islam than out of the traditional historical churches.

"There is a growing awareness among evangelical churches

that if you don't work among the Muslims, your church will die. The Muslim believers in the church are really the key, because they can reach their own people. And that's where we want to work, equipping Muslims who come to know the Lord to reach their people as much as we can. We have been working with four Muslim believers who are already well into their ministry."

At the same time, even in Jerusalem, Muslim believers keep a low profile.

"At least half of the Muslim believers in our congregation are women. One is married but has never told her husband, three are married men who have not told their wives, and the rest are single men and women. If a woman is a Muslim believer and her husband is not and he finds out, he will almost certainly divorce her. And if a husband is a Muslim believer and his wife finds out, she will tell her family and that will cause big problems for him."

Having talked with brethren in the West Bank and Gaza Strip, we were eager to learn what life is like for evangelical Palestinian Christians in the City of Peace.

First of all, Jack explained, Westerners have to understand the caste system in Israel.

"An Israeli Jew is the uppermost class. Second is an Israeli who is not a Jew but came from outside and became a citizen, for example, a Christian Russian or Ethiopian or other nationality. Third class is an Israeli Arab who lives in the north – Druze and others besides Israeli Jews who, though not required to serve in the army, can volunteer and receive all kinds of privileges from that. Fourth class would be an Israeli Arab who lives in Haifa or Nazareth. Fifth class are people from abroad who are not Arabs but who are living here – Greeks or some other nationality. They have an Israeli identity card but are foreign nationals, not Israeli citizens. The Sixth class is the people who live in Jerusalem. They are Arabs but have Israeli identity cards. The Seventh class is people from the West Bank. Eighth class would be people from the Gaza Strip.

"The government treats us according to our class, which is

based on who we are and where we live. You see a big difference, for example, when you walk from Jewish West Jerusalem to Arab East Jerusalem. Outside the Ministry of Interior in East Jerusalem, you will usually see at least 300 people queued up for hours to renew an ID or apply for social services. If I applied there for a work permit, I might be rejected just because I am an Arab. None of this happens at the Interior Ministry on the Israeli side.

"When we walk in West Jerusalem and they recognize us as Arabs, they will stop us, even though we have Israeli citizenship. They might search us. They will look at our IDs. They will ask about us, and then they might just release us. An Arab cannot travel all over Jerusalem as freely as an Israeli. Even at a checkpoint, an Israeli with Israeli tags on his car, can drive around the line of cars and pass through and nobody would stop him or question him. Arabs are always under suspicion. Even evangelical Palestinian Christians who don't have anything to do with all this struggle are suspected as bombers or terrorists.

"So the Palestinian asks, why do I have to go through this? And every day the anger is reinforced and the hurt continues and the depression goes deeper.

"Even as evangelical believers, we find ourselves between two people. We are Israelis. But at the same time, we are Palestinians. And Palestinians are in struggle with the Israelis. So where do we fit? Are we to struggle with them against the Israeli occupation, or are we just to stand by ourselves and say that we have nothing to do with what's going on?

"Many take the second option, and that makes them suspicious to the Muslims or political activists. 'Why are you not struggling with us against the occupation? You are Arabs, you are Palestinians like us, you speak the same language. Why are you not?'

"So we are pressured to say, yes, I want to do something. I want to be part of this. And many believers struggle with their identity. They start identifying too much with the Palestinians. They start compromising their views about loving their enemies. They start approving of things that are not really biblical at all, just because they feel the need to identify.

"As a pastor, I have to address all of this. Walking the hard road has to start with me, because I have the same struggles. I see in the news that my people are being killed, their houses destroyed. And I have to deal with my emotions, with the anger and frustration.

"Labib called me at 8:30 this morning and asked me to meet you here at 9:30. I told him it was impossible because there are checkpoints that hinder me from moving. At the checkpoint, I am insulted so much. My car is checked. I am checked. I am suspect. It really gets me angry when I stand there for two hours just doing nothing, waiting for this guy to check me. I know I have nothing. I have no bombs. I have nothing in my car. It's just a process that makes life harder for me. And we sometimes go through that several times a day.

"I didn't go through the checkpoint this morning. I went the long way, around the settlements, because I didn't want to arrive here frustrated and angry and spoil our visit.

"So it has to start in me. I have to have the peace of the Lord to fill me. And I have to have his love, even for this soldier who will insult me. Without his Holy Spirit, it just would not work.

"When this current intifada started, I preached a sermon. 'This will end,' I told my congregation. 'It's not going to be forever. But we have two choices. Either we surrender to the situation and end up like anybody living in the country – in depression and suffering and hurt and anger and apart from the Lord. Or we choose to live for the Lord and not compromise what we believe, even though it is so hard. Then, at the end, we can say that we have truly conquered in the strength of the Lord.'"

But the intifada and the resulting Israeli retaliation are not the only challenges facing evangelical believers in Jerusalem. The historical churches perceive them as traitors and "sheep stealers." Some of the traditional churches are so small that losing even one family could threaten its existence.

"Historical churches also accuse us of being Zionist, because some of the missionaries who come here from the West are Zionist. Most of my American friends come and boast about being for Israel, and they support Israel and approve of what Israel is doing in the West Bank. So here comes an evangelical brother (me) who wants to serve his people, and I automatically have the stigma of being a Zionist. Can I deny my association with the evangelical churches? I cannot. Can I deny that the evangelical churches in the West support Israel? I cannot. Even though I am not a Zionist and do not approve of what Israel is doing in the country, my brothers are and do. And that puts us in the same family. So the accusation is very supportable.

"For many years, I have been hurt so much, more by my brothers in the West than by Israel. And this is common throughout the evangelical churches in Palestine. We do not ask the churches in America to give us money. We just want them to identify with us and allow us to identify with them. And if not identify, at least feel with us. Say you understand us. On the contrary, many of the brothers from outside come to us with judgment. They even come with rebuke.

"We feel cut off, alone, away from the church. We want to be part of the church worldwide."

As we talk with Jack, we hear his heart and his pain. It is important for us to understand both. Our Palestinian brothers and sisters are not one-dimensional, any more than we are. They too are complex, sometimes even contradictory, children of God — dealing with issues, readjusting focus, repenting, rejoicing, starting over again, hanging on.

"The church here is growing," Jack said. "Our people are growing in the Lord, in maturity and in number. Not as rapidly as in the West, but we have more to deal with here, more opposition, more spiritual pressure than in the West.

"You can feel a spirit of heaviness when you enter the Old City, the spirit of the enemy, tension, a very strong religious spirit. This is a great obstacle that makes life slower and harder.

"The Lord walked here. He cried over this city. One day, the city will bring a smile to His face, when the Body of Christ is united."

*   *   *   *

After Jack Sara left, I felt that this would be a good time to introduce Ron to the Old City. The following are his thoughts and impressions.

I was already on sensory overload. Images, impressions and sensations were coming too fast for me to comprehend, categorize and file. My mind and emotions were constantly considering new issues and concepts and rethinking old ones.

We entered the city through the Jaffa Gate in the westernmost wall, between the Christian and Armenian Quarters.

Jaffa Gate (*Sha'ar Yafo*), I later learned, was built by Turkish Sultan Suleiman, known as "the Magnificent," and is so named because the road to the seacoast port of Jaffa once began here. The road from this gate also went to Hebron, which is why Arabs call it *Bab al-Khalil* (Gate of the Beloved), referring to Abraham who is buried in Hebron. Germany's Kaiser Wilhelm rode through it on horseback, and Britain's General Allenby marched his troops through. Jordan shut it down in 1948, until Israel reopened it 1967.

Tourist shops are clustered just inside the gate. The Tower of David (Song of Songs 4:4) is off to the right.

We hadn't time to properly explore, plus it was the Sabbath, so a lot of shops, restaurants and tourist sites were closed. There was still a good deal of traffic, but it was nothing, Jack informed me, compared to what it had been like before the intifada exploded and stopped the tourist flow.

I wanted to buy gifts for Annie and the kids, so we wound our way through the warren of streets and alleys in the Muslim Quarter. In some ways, it reminded me of the markets of Tijuana, Mexico, where nothing has a price tag, barter is the order of the day and no matter how good the deal, you still pay many times what it's worth.

In other ways, it was a statement of life during the intifada. Jack and I were the only two tourists in sight. Again and again, I listened to the hardship stories of the shopkeepers – much of which, no doubt, was part of the standard Middle Eastern sales patter. But rows of closed shops whose owners had gone out of business testified truly to the hard times caused by the loss of trade.

Jack waited patiently as I bartered, left a shop, was called back, bartered, left, returned, etc., and finally left the Quarter with almost everything I needed. Knowing how real their hardships were, I really didn't mind overpaying.

Mostly, we just wandered around, and I soaked up impressions. We walked along the top of a length of city wall, and I wondered, as every visitor must wonder, whether Jesus or the disciples ever walked or touched any of these ancient stones. Jack told me that the pavement that Jesus walked on was actually about 40 feet beneath us, because Jerusalem, like cities all over Israel, has been built, razed and rebuilt time and again. The countryside was different, he explained. The sand along the Galilee could be the same that stuck between the Lord's toes.

In addition to the Muslim Quarter, I have two other vivid memories of our visit to the Old City.

The first is the Western Wall. I couldn't take my eyes off it. At the entrance was a kiosk with a box of kippahs. Jack waited out on the plaza as I put one on my head and walked slowly to the wall, savoring the moment. It was one of those I-can't-believe-I'm-really-here experiences that grew stronger, almost painfully wonderful, as I approached the stones.

Once within reach, I stood, studying every crack and fissure. Tiny slips of paper were stuffed into every opening. On each was written somebody's prayer. Out of the corner of my eye, I saw an Ashkenazi Jew with his distinctive costume and *payos* (side curls) step up to a space to my right and immediately begin to bob and chant as I had seen often in documentaries and travelogues.

For a while, I stayed and prayed, letting images and memories flood in . . . decades of singing and dancing and praying with Jewish believers in messianic synagogues in the States . . . playing Jewish music on my guitar, music in the minor keys that did not allow anyone who heard keep his feet still – music in whose notes wailed the history of countless generations of Jews . . . faces of Jewish friends who had made *aliya* (return to the Land) five years ago and now lived in the north around Kiriat Ata, some of whom I hoped to see before we left.   And now, swirling through these memories, the faces of new Palestinian friends.

Standing there at the base of the Second Temple, I was certain, as Jack Sara had said, that Jesus still wept over Jerusalem.

The other memory I hold of the Old City is of sitting with Jack outside a small Arab restaurant at the entrance to the Muslim Quarter.   As we relaxed with a cold drink, we saw a group of *yeshivot* (Jewish students) – black slacks, white shirts, black hats, payos, and tallit (prayer shawls) – each carrying a Galil assault rifle.

The weapons looked out of place for these young religious students walking and talking and laughing together, just as young people do the world over.   They were headed for the mouth of the Muslim Quarter.   Suddenly, as if responding to some unseen cue or telepathic understanding, they reached into their pockets and pulled out ammunition clips. A series of harsh clicks stabbed the warm spring air as they loaded the rounds and entered the Quarter.

Were they intentionally trying to provoke trouble?   Were they flaunting their power and privilege?   Was the road through the Muslim Quarter the only way to their synagogue?

Like the Wailing Wall, these yeshiva students were symbols to me.

The wall represented the promise of the Old Covenant and the fulfillment of the New.   It stood as a testimony of God's relationship with His people – His blessings when they obey, his chastisement when they don't.

The students warned of the future. Of another generation of Jews already going to their Arab brothers with fingers on the triggers. And somewhere deep in the labyrinth of the Muslim Quarter there might be a young man or woman who already has all of the anger or hopelessness needed to strap on a belt of explosives and walk down the streets of the Jewish Quarter.

God forbid that the epitaph of both Jew and Arab would be that of so many of Israel's monarchs who, generation after generation "did evil in the eyes of the Lord, as his fathers had done" (2 Kings 15:9).

*   *   *   *

Reluctantly, we finally left the Old City, went to dinner and, in the evening, stopped by IMS offices to talk with our audio/video director, Waleed Rishmawi (Wah-leed' Rish-mah'-wee).

A graduate of Bob Jones University in the States, Waleed lives in Bethlehem with his brother and sister-in-law and their two children. Their home is just off Manger Square near the Church of the Nativity. For weeks, he had been unable to leave his house to come to work.

"The first day of the siege," Waleed recalled, "two Apache helicopters flew over our house, firing into the church with 750 mm shells. My niece and nephew were so scared that they clung to my legs. My seven-year-old niece still has nightmares. All through the night for a month, she listened to grenades and heavy machine guns, every single night.

"My second cousin was killed by Israeli soldiers. He owned a four-story apartment building, and one day he got a call that he needed to come over because soldiers were about to blow open the door. So he drove down to find three tanks sitting there. When he saw the tanks, he turned around to leave. But the tank gunners saw him, and they shot him. When an ambulance came and tried to rescue him, the soldiers shot at the ambulance. Finally, they stopped shooting, and the medical people took him to a house nearby. When they entered the house, the very old lady who lived there saw the bloody corpse, had a heart attack and died."

Waleed is deeply concerned for his cousin's son, because he is so filled with hatred.

" 'Waleed,' he told me angrily, 'my dad was not in politics, he was not a terrorist, he never carried a gun in his life. They just killed him in cold blood.'

"Revenge is part of the Middle East culture. If I shoot you, your brother will avenge your death. They cannot let go of offenses. They have to do something about it. To shake the hand of your enemy in the Middle East is a sign of weakness. To me, as a believer, to shake the hand of my enemy is a sign of strength, because it's easy to kill him, but it's not easy to forgive. Once you forgive, that's strength. That's courage."

Despite the cultural norms, however, Waleed is convinced that reconciliation and peaceful coexistence are possible. And he saw clear evidence of it recently on a return flight from the United States – seated next to an Israeli settler.

"When we introduced ourselves, I didn't tell him I was Palestinian. We just shook hands and talked. When the food came, we prayed together. I prayed in English instead of Arabic, and when I used the name of Jesus, he knew I was Christian and assumed I was not Palestinian.

"We talked for about four hours about soccer, politics, the chosen people, the Promised Land, you name it. And we kept on talking during a one-hour layover in Cyprus.

"At one point, he looked at me and said, 'You know what? I like you. You're a nice guy.' So I said, 'You know what? I like you too.' And we kept on talking like there was nothing between us, like we were not Palestinian Arab and Israeli Jew.

" 'Do you have kids?' I asked him.

" 'Yes,' he said, as we ate together. We *had bread and salt*, as we say in Arabic.

"Then he said, 'You know what? I know the Palestinians are teaching their kids to hate us. But we're doing the same thing.'

" 'So you think that's going to bring peace to the land?'

" 'No, but we have to teach our kids the true religion. And this is our land, given by the Lord.'

" 'Do you know the Lord?'

And he said no, so we talked about that for five minutes.

When the plane landed, I went to get my luggage and leave. But first, I said, 'By the way, I'm Waleed Rishmawi, and I'm from Bethlehem.' And I watched his jaw drop.

" 'You didn't tell me you're Palestinian?'

" 'So, what now?'

" 'Well, I heard some rumors about you Palestinians. I heard that a good Palestinian is a dead Palestinian. Now I know it's wrong.'

" 'Yes, and I heard the same thing about you settlers. So what are we going to do about it?'

" 'From now on,' he said, 'I'm going to change the attitude of my children and tell them that there are good Palestinians.'

" 'And I'll be doing the same thing. When I get married and have kids, I'll tell them that there are good Israelis. And change will begin with us.' "

This was not Waleed's first encounter with reconciliation. The first came during a Musalaha desert encounter.

"I was stuck on a camel with a Jew, and I wondered what I was going to say. Well, I found out that he speaks English and I speak English. He plays soccer, and I play soccer. So it was a starting point.

"At the end of the three-hour trip on a camel, he said, 'Let me be honest with you. When I got on that camel with you, I didn't like you. The minute I knew I was sitting beside an Arab, hatred was in my heart. But when I found something in common with you, when we shared our problems with one another and got to know each other so well, I asked the Lord to take that hatred away, to make it dissolve and give me peace instead. And I think peace is happening right now between you and me.'

"Since then, we've been good friends. The last time we saw each other, we had steak in Haifa."

Just as the ministry of Musalaha encourages and facilitates forgiveness and reconciliation between Jewish and Arab believers, we pray that this book will encourage and facilitate understanding and love between American and Arab believers.

"We wake up in the morning and have breakfast like Christians in the U.S.," Waleed said. "We go through difficult times like they do. We love the Lord as much as they do. And we need them to be with us, not against us. I don't have a problem with any Christians supporting Israel with money or prayers. I don't mind that. I just encourage them to look at the other side and to recognize that there are Palestinian believers too.

"But the only emails I receive from Christians in America say that Palestinians are terrorists and need to be killed. A Christian church in America even donated money for a tank. Imagine how we felt as we watched the news and saw a tank crossing over on shipboard to Israel with a big sign on it reading, 'Donated by the Christians of the United States.'

"Most Palestinians do not support terrorism. A few become terrorists because they think it's the only way they can change the situation. Israelis have bad ones; Palestinians have bad ones. And Arafat is between the two, stuck between two fires, as we say in Arabic."

Yasser Arafat is not the only one who is stuck between two fires. Evangelical Palestinian Christians are stuck between a world aflame with hatred, violence and vengeance on one side and on the other side, the Kingdom of God, burning more brightly than the sun with his unquenchable love.

*   *   *   *

ITEM: In Tel Aviv tonight, an estimated 150,000 people gathered for what some are calling the largest peace rally since the beginning of the intifada. Banners in Hebrew called for "Two states for two peoples" and pleaded with the government to "Leave the territories for the sake of Israel." At the end of the rally, everyone sang the national anthem, *Hatikva*, which means "The Hope":

> In the Jewish heart,
> A Jewish spirit still sings,
> And the eyes look east
> Toward Zion.
> Our hope is not lost,
> Our hope of two thousand years,
> To be a free nation in our land,
> In the land of Zion and Jerusalem.

They yearn for their own land, yes, but many are willing to share it.

May 12

Jesus replied: "Love the Lord your God with all your heart and with all your soul and with all your mind." This is the first and greatest commandment. And the second is like it: "Love your neighbor as yourself." All the Law and the Prophets hang on these two commandments. Matthew 22:37-40

ITEM: Defense Minister Binyamin Ben-Eliezer decided last night to postpone the IDF incursion into Gaza.

Things appeared to be relatively calm this morning. After breakfast, Ron and I returned to the Old City to worship with Labib and his family at Jack Sara's church.

This time, we entered through the Damascus Gate in the middle of the north wall, which leads directly down El Wad road into the Muslim Quarter.

We walked through residential areas and the open marketplace, instead of running the gauntlet of shops and stalls. The sounds and sights seemed to be right out of an old movie. The air was heady with deliciously exotic smells of cinnamon, saffron and thick Arab coffee.

Over the past week, we had talked and "shared bread and salt" with our Palestinian brothers and sisters. Today, we worshiped with them.

The ground-level rooms of the Jerusalem Alliance Church were named after the four evangelists. Each designated an age group for children's church. Adults met together in a large upper room that opened onto the roof.

The worship service was in Arabic and, though we understood nothing, we experienced a sweet unity far deeper than shared language or custom.

"Music," Longfellow said, "is the universal language of mankind."

"Speak to one another with psalms, hymns and spiritual songs," Paul instructed. "Sing and make music in your heart to the Lord, always giving thanks to God the Father for everything, in the name of our Lord Jesus Christ" (Ephesians 5).

We did and were blessed.

Following the service we drove to Beit Jala, another suburb of Bethlehem, for a final visit before returning to Tel Aviv and catching our flight home.

The area had changed little since our last visit. The IDF troops were gone, but the scars and much of the debris remained. This time, however, we were able to drive through the Israeli checkpoint, instead of sneaking in the back way through the mountains.

*   *   *   *

Carlo and Ida Ghubar (Guh-bar') are the soon-to-be in-laws of our friend Wa'el Hashwa in Gaza City. He is engaged to their daughter, Patricia. [Two months after we returned from our research trip, Pastor Hanna married Wa'el and Patricia in Jordan. They now live in Gaza – jk]

Carlo is a native of Beit Jala. He studied mining engineering in Yugoslavia and became a believer after three years of marriage to Ida.

"Some women came to our home and talked to my wife about Jesus. Then they invited us to go to the church. We went, but I went only to laugh at them.

"I did not laugh, though.

"I felt something different there. The atmosphere was different. I had never felt it before. Then the pastor preached about God's Son, and I actually saw Jesus standing beside him. Jesus opened his hand and motioned toward me. 'Come to Me, son,' He said, 'I am waiting for you.'

" 'Waiting for me?' I told the Lord. 'I don't need You. I don't believe in You, and You wait for me?' "

" 'Yes, I am waiting for you.' "

Carlo, Patricia and Ida Ghubar in their home in Beit Jala, shortly after the end of the Bethlehem siege.

"I saw a kind of love in His eyes that I cannot forget. You can't imagine that love. Then I lifted my face, went running down to His feet, asked Him to forgive me and began to cry. That was in 1978, and from that time, I have gone with Jesus."

Twenty years later, Labib invited Carlo to serve as an evangelist with the Bible Society in Gaza City. He wanted to open a bookstore there.

"People tried to discourage me. They tried to make me afraid of going to Gaza. 'Gaza is mostly Muslim fanatics,' they said. 'They will kill you. They will crush the place.'

"So Labib and I prayed for about a month and a half. During that time, Jesus told me from Isaiah 45 that he would open the doors and make the hills level for me. So I went.

"The bookstore opened in 1999, and the people in Gaza welcomed us. They were not against us. And after several months there, a Muslim came and asked me about Jesus. He sat with me for nine or ten hours that day, and we talked. Then he said he wanted to give himself to Jesus. After we prayed, he didn't want to leave me. He wanted to ask more and more about Jesus."

This new believer was proved to be only the first fruits of Carlo's ministry.

"We did not have to go outside to find the people. God sent them to us and they asked about Jesus. We saw their thirst. It's something we could not even imagine before that. And most of them were from the fanatic Islamic University."

For the next three years, Carlo served in Gaza, making monthly trips to Beit Jala to be with his family. Then the intifada began.

Labib pulled Carlo out of Gaza and sent him to the northern portion of the West Bank, to Nablus, to open a bookstore there.

After Carlo returned home, he was invited by the Palestinian Ministry of Culture to serve at the international book fair in the Islamic Sultanate of Oman. Oman is home to only a handful of indigenous believers. The rest of the tiny minority Christian population is made up of expatriates. Most others are Muslim.

At the bookfair, Carlo exhibited his stock of religious books in the official Palestinian section, marking the first time that the Bible has been displayed publicly in Oman (outside the church compounds).

"Many people had never seen the Bible before," Carlo told us. "Some asked questions about Jesus." Even the Omani authorities and the Palestinian ambassador to Oman were very positive about the Bible Society display.

During the two-week exhibition in Oman, the IDF laid siege to Bethlehem, Beit Sahour and Beit Jala. Carlo returned to Jordan, trusting the Lord to help him get back to his family.

"I prayed that God would let me know whether to stay in Jordan or whether he would make it safe for me to return to my family. In the morning, I went to the Allenby Bridge that crosses over the Jordan River into Jericho. It was open. I had my answer. Some of my neighbors were there, worried about how they would get home.

" 'Come with me,' I said. 'It will be easy. Don't worry.' "

"We crossed the bridge into Jericho and took a car to a village near Jerusalem. There I found a taxi driver who was willing to risk his life to bring us into the siege area, despite the 24-hour curfew. The whole way in, we never saw one Israeli. That was a miracle.

" 'How can you *do* that?" my neighbors wanted to know.

" 'Nobody can see us,' I said. 'That's from God, not from me.' "

"The driver brought me right to my door and took my neighbors to their homes also.

"Since then, we have been here, surrounded, unable to go anywhere. We prayed. We sang. We did not fear as the other people feared, because we trusted God to protect us. And if He did not protect us, that would be good too. Then we would be with Him. Either way, we would be with Him.

"One day, we heard the sounds of the tanks coming down our street to search houses. The search stopped two houses from ours. The soldiers never searched our home.

"An elderly sister in our church told us of a time when she opened her front door ten minutes before the curfew was supposed to be lifted (every once in a while, the soldiers lifted the curfew for a couple of hours to allow people to buy whatever food and medicine that was available). She just wanted to look out. Three bullets hit the door before she could close it again."

During more than 850 hours of curfew, Bethlehem's 130,000 residents, including 90,000 children, were allowed out of their homes for only 16 hours.[1]

Although Carlo's work in Gaza and Nablus are on hold, God keeps him and his family busy in Bethlehem.

"Our ministry is to help our neighbors, to speak with them about Jesus and also to help them financially if we can. Brother Labib sent us some donated money so that we could help our neighbors when the Israelis lifted the curfew."

The siege gave Palestinians in Bethlehem a lot of time to think. When it ended, some came to Carlo and his family to ask questions. And strange to see in this little town where Jesus was born, most of those inquiring after him were Muslims.

Notes

[1] Matthew Gutman, "What in God's name am I doing here?" (*The Jerusalem Post*, Monday, May 20, 2002).

Conclusion

Now you are the body of Christ, and
each one of you is a part of it. 1 Corinthians
12:27

Within these pages, you have met some of your Palestinian
brothers and sisters. You have seen their faces and shared their
hearts.

What now?

You have already taken the first step. By taking the time to
read this book, you have begun the process of identifying with our
Palestinian brothers and sisters.

"The body is a unit" Paul said, "though it is made up of many
parts; and though all its parts are many, they form one body. So it
is with Christ. For we were all baptized by one Spirit into one
body—whether Jews or Greeks, slave or free—and we were all
given the one Spirit to drink. . . . If one part [of the body of Christ]
suffers, every part suffers with it" (1 Corinthians 12:12-13,26).

As unique members of the same body, we are encouraged to
"Rejoice with those who rejoice; mourn with those who mourn
(Romans 12:15). These are days of deep mourning, days when we
should share in the suffering of our brethren in Palestine

Deeper than identifying with one another, we need to enter
into unity with one another in Christ – Jewish believers with Arab
believers with American believers – to let the world know that the
Father sent Jesus and has loved them even as He has loved His own
Son (John 17:23).

As we identify with one another and come into unity, it will be natural for us to carry each other's burdens and in this way fulfill the law of Christ (Galatians 6:2).

We can do this in two key ways. We can pray, and we can act.

Prayer and Intercession

"Pray for the peace of Jerusalem: 'May those who love you be secure. May there be peace within your walls and security within your citadels.' For the sake of my brothers and friends, I will say, 'Peace be within you.' For the sake of the house of the Lord our God, I will seek your prosperity" (Psalm 122:6-9).

Jerusalem is home both to Jews and to Arabs. When we pray for the peace of the city, we pray for reconciliation between enemies. This kind of praying is the greatest contribution that you can make. The effective prayer of a righteous man can accomplish much.

Please visit our website www.bannerc.com to find more information and specific prayer needs for the people of the region. You can also connect with other prayer efforts for the Middle East and North Africa by visiting www.WIN1040.com.

Meeting Material Needs

"Let us not become weary in doing good, for at the proper time we will reap a harvest if we do not give up. Therefore, as we have opportunity, let us do good to all people, *especially to those who belong to the family of believers*" (Galatians 6:9-10).

The church in Palestine needs short-term missionaries to teach drama and puppetry for children's ministries, to train musicians for worship and to help raise up new leaders.

Palestinian pastors need hugs, prayers, strength and encouragement from Western pastors who are not drained, as they are, from their daily struggles. Evangelical congregations need financial help to buy food, medicine and other necessities, not only for their own families but also as a demonstration of God's love to their

Muslim neighbors. And when we give, let us give as brothers blessing brothers, not as the rich stepping down to the poor, for we share the same Father who is the source of all blessing.

"What good is it, my brothers, if a man claims to have faith but has no deeds? Can such faith save him? Suppose a brother or sister is without clothes and daily food. If one of you says to him, 'Go, I wish you well; keep warm and well fed,' but does nothing about his physical needs, what good is it?" (James 2:14-16).

You can adopt a family. You can demonstrate immediate compassion to a Palestinian family living in the West Bank with a gift of $200.00. This will provide a family of four with the basic necessities of food, produce, water and electricity, medicine, clothes, wintertime heating, and hygienic needs, such as detergent and soap. A smaller or larger gift will also make a difference for these families living under conditions of desperate poverty. Please give from your heart as God directs you.

You are welcome to make your gift through Banner Communications and it will be immediately transferred to help the families. Banner Communications is a non-profit 501(c)(3) organization and can give tax-deductible receipts. Please specify that your gift is for **Adopt a Family**.

Tell children about Jesus. In the only outreach of its kind in the Palestinian Territories, our partnership with the Bible Society is sharing the love and peace of Jesus with more than 50,000 children and young people. More than 35 communities are already participating in this program and the number continues to grow. This is our most strategic ministry to the Palestinian society and one that will help change the future of these people. Your financial support will help us staff the ministry, cover transportation costs, and provide needed equipment and materials. Again, please specify that your gift is for **Tell the Children**, and your gift will be directed toward this effort.

Be a monthly partner. Of the $120 billion annually funded to Christian mission agencies worldwide, the entire Middle East, which takes in all the countries in the region, receives less than $80 million, or less than seven-tenths of one percent, for any Christian outreach. Your monthly commitment as a **partner in ministry** can help correct this imbalance, and more importantly, share God's love with more people. By sharing each month the amount God places in your heart, you will help provide a more solid financial foundation, by which we can more consistently carry out our compassionate outreach in the Middle East.

The unique ministry of Banner Communications

Our spiritual birthplace waits in darkness for the Light of Life. The region of the Middle East and North Africa has a population of 450 million people and is growing by 1,000,000 each month. Only five percent of the entire region is Christian. This includes Orthodox, Catholic, Coptic, Evangelical and all other expressions of Christianity.

There is very little access in the region to Christian resource material. Only 0.6% of worldwide mission resources and 1.1% of worldwide missionaries go to the Middle East and North Africa. It only receives 1% of the world's Bibles and of the $3 billion spent each year on Christian media, only 0.1% (one-tenth of one percent) is spent in the Middle East.

Banner Communications is working to help change that imbalance. A 52 program video series on the life of Jesus Christ called the "Light of Life" and a 52 program series on the Gospel of John called the "Gospel of Belief" have been produced in the Arabic language and culture. Both series are shot on location in Israel and both series are being broadcast on the SAT-7 Arab language satellite network and in the Sudan on the national TV network there.

The series are unique because they are also developed into video discipleship packets with a written study guide and are distributed to believers and churches throughout the entire Middle East and North Africa. The Gospel of Matthew, entitled "The Gospel of the King" will soon go into production followed by the 52-part series on the life, teaching and travels of the Apostle Paul.

The strategy driving the whole effort is first to communicate to the masses through satellite broadcast, and second, to use the same material on the ground to reach the individual and, ultimately, provide a thorough curriculum for Christian leadership and discipleship development. Partnership with indigenous and credible ministries already working in the region is the key to the great success of the ministry.

Discipleship Packet: A gift of $169.00 will provide a church or group of Believers in Israel, the West Bank, and throughout the Middle East and North Africa with the entire 52-episode "The Life of Christ" program series on VHS videocassette, plus 10 study guide manuals. Your gift will help disciple Arab believers, strengthen their churches and, ultimately, impact many more lives with the love and peace of Jesus Christ.

The following ministries are on the front lines, making incredible sacrifices and doing a great work for the Kingdom of God. I strongly encourage you to pray for them, support them, contact and encourage them.

If you would like to support these international ministries directly through Banner Communications ministry in order to receive a tax receipt, you are welcome. Your gift will be transferred directly to them.

Bethlehem Bible College
P.O. Box 127
Bethlehem, W.B., Israel
www.bethbc@planet.edu

Sat-7 Arabic Language
Christian Satellite Net
P.O. Box 26760
CY-1647 Nicosia, Cyprus
www.SAT-7.org

Window International Network
P.O. Box 4927
Colorado Springs, CO 80949
www.WIN1040.com

The Palestinian Bible Society
P.O. Box 19627
91196 Jerusalem, Israel
www.Biblesoc@netvision.net.il

Musalaha Ministries
P.O. Box 52110
91521 Jerusalem, Israel
www.musalaha@netvision.net.il

Sat-7 North America
P.O. Box 113
Wayne, PA 19087-0113

If you would like to know more about a church or pastor in this book in order to pray more effectively for them and/or support them, please contact us.

"If anyone has material possessions and sees his brother in need but has no pity on him. How can the love of God be in him? Dear children, let us not love with words or tongue but with actions and in truth" (1 John 3:17-18 NIV) Please respond prayerfully to the needs of the Palestinians and other Arab Christians today.

For more information, please write to us at Banner Communications, Inc., 9417 NW 43rd Street, Suite D-4, Gainesville, FL 32653, or fill out and return the form at the back of this book.

Epilogue

In a feature article entitled "Code Blue in Jerusalem" in the July 1, 2002 issue of *Newsweek* magazine, correspondents Joshua Hammer and Joanna Chen paint a grisly portrait of the carnage of suicide bombings from the perspective of hospital emergency rooms.

Reflecting the despair felt by many of his countrymen, *Ha'aretz* columnist Ari Shavit was quoted as saying, "There is this feeling, 'We tried politics, we tried the Army, we tried everything.' What's left?"

In the West Bank and Gaza Strip, Arabs too are asking, "What's left?"

And only our brothers and sisters in Palestine and Israel can give them the answer.

**"How beautiful are the feet of those
who bring good news!"** (Romans 10:15)

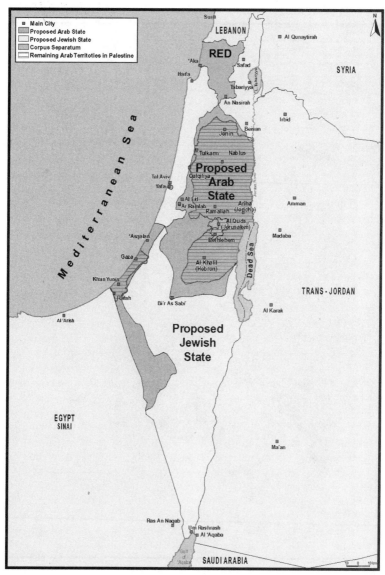

The United Nations Partition Plan, 1947. (Applied Research Institute-Jerusalem (ARIJ), reprinted by permission of the Bethlehem Bible College.)

Depopulated Palestinian Villages in 1948 and 1967. (ARIJ, reprinted by permission of the Bethlehem Bible College.)

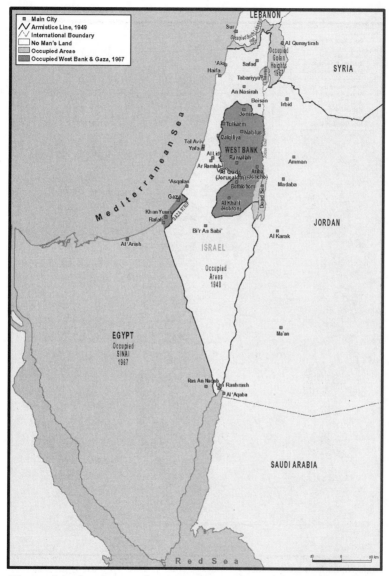

Wars and border changes after 1967. (ARIJ, reprinted by permission of the Bethlehem Bible College.)

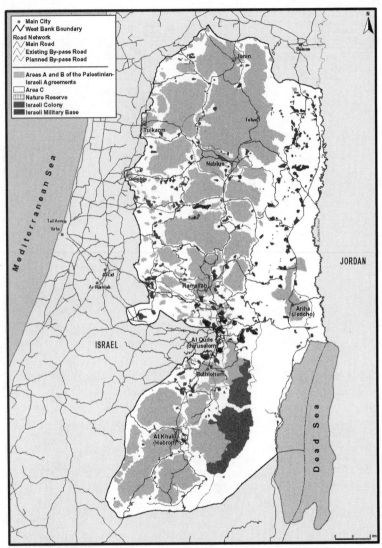

Palestinian land under Israeli occupation, 2000. (ARIJ, reprinted by permission of the Bethlehem Bible College.)

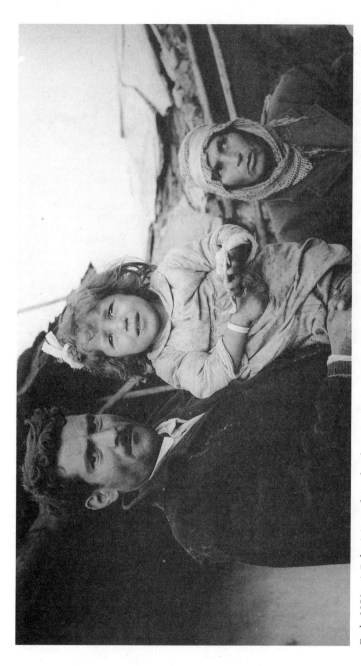

Early 1950s. A Palestinian refugee family waits to receive a tent at a United Nations emergency distribution center after the severe winter storm damaged their makeshift shelter. (United Nations Relief and Works Agency (UNRWA) photo taken by Myrtle Winter-Chaumony, reprinted by permission.)

In 1967, thousands of Palestinians, young and old, fled over the Allenby Bridge from Jericho over the Jordan River to find refuge in Jordan, and many became refugees for the second time in their lives. Most were unable to return to their homes in the West Bank and Gaza Strip which were occupied by Israel after the 1967 war. (UNRWA photo by George Nehmeh, reprinted by permission.)

Baqa'a camp was one of the ten tented emergency camps established by the UNRWA after the 1967 Arab/Israeli war, when tens of thousands of people became refugees. Today, Baqa'a has a refugee population of over 75,000. (UNRWA photo by George Nehmeh, reprinted by permission.)

Palestinian refugees in 1967, crossing the Allenby Bridge. (Courtesy of the Israeli Government Press Office, photo by Eldan David.)

Palestinian refugees in 1967, leaving their hiding places under the eyes of a unit of the Israeli Border Police. (Courtesy of the Israeli Government Press Office, photo by Kanper Aryeh.)

Israeli tanks in the West Bank, November 2001. (Photo by Jamal Arouri, reprinted by permission of the Palestinian Bible Society.)

Destroyed houses in the Jenin refugee camp in the West Bank after the Israeli withdrawal, ending Operation Defensive Shield. Hospital officials reported receiving 42 bodies, while IDF spokesmen said 23 soldiers had been killed, April 2002. (USRWA, reprinted by permission.)

بسم الله الرحمن الرحيم
"من المؤمنين رجال صدقوا ما عاهدوا الله عليه فمنهم من قضى نحبه ومنهم من ينتظر وما بدلوا تبديلا"

حركة التحرير الوطني الفلسطيني - فتح
تحتسب عند الله شهيد الوطن و الواجب الإنساني
(شهيد انتفاضة الأقصى)

الشهيد البطل الدكتور الصيدلاني
(مدير مستشفى اليمامة التخصصي - الخضر)

احمد نعمان عثمان (أبو نعمان)

الذي استشهد على ارض مدينة الخضر الصامدة أثناء اقتحام
محافظة بيت لحم يوم الجمعة ٢٠٠٢/٣/٨
اثر اغتيال وحشي من قبل الاحتلال الصهيوني الغاشم
المجد والخلود لشهدائنا الابرار

Posters like this virtually paper outside walls and doors throughout the West Bank and Gaza Strip. This man was a doctor who was shot leaving his home during the seige of the Church of the Nativity in Bethlehem, April 2002.

Appendix I

Who Hates More? Who Is More Evil?
Salim J. Munayer, Ph.D.

[The following article is reprinted because it provides the reader with a clearer and deeper understanding of the ongoing conflict between Israelis and Palestinians and demonstrates that the only hope for peace is reconciliation through Jesus Christ, the hope for which all Christians worldwide are encouraged to fervently pray. – The Authors.]

Last week, in the space of 24 hours, both the Israeli and Palestinian people experienced the loss of children as a result of the ongoing conflict. The Israeli media had full-time coverage of the murder of two Israeli schoolboys. Israeli government representatives went on in length, describing the atrocities committed and blaming the Palestinian Authority for inciting and supporting such violent acts. The Palestinian media had full-time coverage of the death of a Palestinian baby, killed by tank fire. Palestinians accused Israelis of having no consideration for Palestinian life. Unfortunately, such accusations re-occur almost every day. Each side blames the other, saying that they have lost all moral and ethical standards. It is more than evident that hatred is a prevailing force on both sides.

Israelis accuse the Palestinians of calling for the death of Jews, bringing quotations from Muslim clergymen's speeches, video and sound clips to prove their point. Israelis charge that children are taught in schools to hate Israel. Palestinians counter with their own charges, quoting the words of the Orthodox Sephardic spiritual leader, who recently called on the army to kill Arabs. They point to the graffiti written on Israeli walls, "Death to Arabs," which is also used as a popular slogan at football games.

At times when an outsider looks at us and our societies, his description can alert us to the severity of our situation. In an interview with *Ha'aretz* newspaper on April 27, a senior photographer from *National Geographic* spoke of the two weeks he spent photographing his travels between Jerusalem and Hebron. In his five visits he perceived the situation growing worse. He noted that he could sense and feel the hatred between people. According to his experience photographing around the world for 20 years, being 100 countries and many war zones, the magnitude of hatred between Palestinians and Israelis was matched only in Rwanda when the Hutu massacred the Tutsi. However, there the hatred was not with the same intellectual or religious connotations.

Scholars engaged in studying and evaluating conflict between groups have observed certain phenomena that can help us to understand some aspects of hatred and prejudice. This article will highlight a few of these trends and look at the Bible's exhortations in the area of hatred.

Trends among groups in conflict

Division between *us* and *them*.

Individuals tend to evaluate one's own group with sensitivity and favor. We are able to understand our own group, recognize its good qualities, and become attached to it. We overlook our own shortcomings because it is important to distinguish between *us* (who are right and good and merciful) and *them* (who are evil and wrong); and thus we can blame them.

Failure to see plurality within other side.

It is more difficult to understand 'them.' Instead of recognizing their qualities, we generalize and stereotype the other, saying things like, 'They all hate and want to kill us,' or 'They are the animals, they are the evil ones.' We are unable to see them as individuals with unique feelings and thoughts.

Palestinians generally view all Israelis as being right-winged and wanting to take their land. They do not recognize that many Israelis are writing and speaking out for peace and compromise. On the other side, Israelis tend to feel that all Palestinians would like to kill them, and do not realize that many Palestinians simply want to live in peace. Jews feel that all Arabs are the same and cannot be trusted. Arabs feel that all Jews are the same and cannot be trusted.

Due to the language barrier, Israelis and Palestinians do not read each other's newspapers and watch their TV programs. Thus they are dependent on very selective information given to them about the other side. One example is when a Western group associated with Holocaust denial wanted to hold an international conference in Lebanon. The conference was cancelled due to the strong protests of Palestinian, other Arab and international scholars and leaders. However, Israeli media focused on the issue of the conference and its supporters, giving little attention to those who blocked the event.

On the other side, when the previously mentioned rabbi cried out for the destruction of Palestinian homes and their death, Palestinians attributed these sentiments to all Jews. They failed to hear the voice of many Israelis condemning the rabbi's words.

While we understand and perhaps accept the variety of feeling and opinion within our own group, we do not recognize the debates and disagreements within the other group. Rather, we see them as one group united together against us.

Moral Superiority.

Thus, we decide that *we* are more peace loving, trustworthy, and honest. Our values become a moral authority, and we view with contempt those who have different values. Often we will not mix with those who do not share our moral standards, as they might change or corrupt us. The feeling of moral superiority allows for separation and protection; and can justify hatred or legitimize mistreatment of *them*.

During the pope's visit to Syria, President Bishar Assad gave an example of this attitude of moral superiority, when he likened the actions of the state of Israel to those of the Nazis; declaring that they are violating all human, moral principles. On the other side, Israeli President Moshe Katsav recently gave a speech where he spoke of a huge gap between us and the enemy [Arabs] in the areas of morality, ethics and conscience, as the Arabs are coming from a "totally different galaxy."

Perceived threat/victimization.

Both Israelis and Palestinian Arabs strongly perceive themselves as victims, and therefore are unable to see themselves as a threat to the other. If we are the victims, then we cannot be the victimizers. The victims' mentality causes them to be blind to others' pain, aspirations and needs, and therefore justify their attitude towards the other. This perception of themselves as the threatened and injured party, also allows for fear and hostility towards the other. Therefore violent action is justified, and some politicians use these fears to promote their political agenda.

Biblical Principles and Response

As Israeli and Palestinian believers we feel and experience with our people the effect of the conflict. Awareness of the dynamics of hatred can help us not to allow hatred to overcome us. Biblical principles can help us in this difficult situation.

"So God created man in his own image," (Gen. 1:27). All people are **created** in God's likeness. Thus, as believers we are not permitted to dehumanize or demonize the other, as all are formed after the image of God. We are commanded to act in love and respect towards all of God's creation.

"For all have sinned and fall short of the glory of God" (Rom.

3:23) **All** of humanity is **fallen** and in need of restoration, regardless of their ethnicity or religious background. The prophet Amos spoke to not one, but many nations on their responsibility for their own sin. Also as individuals it is clear that "At one time we too were foolish, disobedient, deceived and enslaved by all kinds of passions and pleasures. We lived in malice and envy, being hated and hating one another" (Titus 3:3). We are all in need redemption from the sin of hatred and restoration through the power of resurrection.

Hatred is a **destructive** sin. In Romans 3:10,14-17, Paul quotes: "There is no one righteous, not even one.... Their mouths are full of cursing and bitterness. Their feet are swift to shed blood; ruin and misery make their ways, and the way of peace they do not know." As believers we should mindful that hatred and hostility leads to violence and murder of those created in God's image. We must be alert, for Jesus warns that in time of trial, "many will turn away from the faith and will betray and hate each other" (Mt. 24:9-11).

We must deal with the sin of hatred **within ourselves** and our people **before judging** others. The blame that we assign to others, our bitterness at their offenses, falls second to the recognition of our own sinful natures. Jesus spoke to individuals, asking us to take a sincere look at ourselves before passing judgment on others. "Why do you look at the speck of sawdust in your brother's eye and pay no attention to the plank in your own eye?" (Mt. 7). We are called to introspection and self-examination before confrontation with others. Before we preach about the other's hatred we much check our own hearts.

How then are we to respond to our enemy? How do we react to hatred? Jesus' answer is clear: "But I tell you: **Love your enemies** and pray for those who persecute you (Mt. 5)." In many conflicts around the world, even believers in Jesus find themselves on opposite sides of the fence. However, we cannot follow God and stay in the darkness of hatred, "Anyone who claims to be in the light but hates his brother is still in the darkness" I John 2:9. Jesus asks us to take more than a passive role. We are prompted to take a stand against evil, and to take action by loving one another and even those who hate us.

Paul instructs us on how to treat one another: "Be devoted to one another in brotherly love. Honor one another above yourselves...Bless those who persecute you; bless and do not curse....Do not repay anyone evil for evil....Do not take revenge, my friends, but leave room for God's wrath...Do not be overcome by evil, but overcome evil with good" (Rom. 12: 9-21).

As humans, to love those who hurt and persecute us is difficult. Thus we rely on the Holy Spirit to help us fulfill God's calling on our lives. "In the same way, the Spirit helps us in our weakness" (Romans 8:26). Although we might be unable to resist the anger, bitterness and hatred that so quickly springs up, we remember that "No, in all these things we are more than conquerors through him who loved us" (Romans 8:37). In this world that preaches revenge, we must stand in radical opposition to the sin of hatred that separates us from God and from each other. "Above all, love each other deeply, for love covers over a multitude of sins" (1 Pet. 4:8).

Sources

Brewer, M.B. (1999) The psychology of prejudice: ingroup love or outgroup hate? Journal of Social Issues.

Ha'aretz Weekend Edition, April 27, 2001.

Stephan, W.G. & Stephan, C.W. (1996). Intergroup relations. Dubuque, IA: Brown & Benchmark.

Reprinted by permission

Appendix II

The Zionism of Man vs. the Zionism of God
Ron Brackin

> Jesus turned and rebuked them. And he said, "You do not know what kind of spirit you are of, for the Son of Man did not come to destroy men's lives, but to save them." (Luke 9:55)

The Zionism of God is God fulfilling his prophecy his way, in his time. The Zionism of Man is man trying to "make it happen."

The Zionism of Man caused Abraham to try to fulfill the Lord's promises through Ishmael. The Zionism of God fulfilled the Lord's promises to Abraham through Isaac.

The Zionism of Man caused David to number his fighting men at the cost of 70,000 Hebrew lives (2 Samuel 24). The Zionism of God led Jehoshaphat to put the praise team at the head of the army and watch the Lord defeat the hordes of Ammon, Moab and Mount Seir (2 Chronicles 20).

Man's Zionism offered Jesus all the kingdoms of the world without the cross (Matthew 4:8-9). God's Zionism led Jesus to the cross, ensuring that the kingdom of the world will become the kingdom of our Lord and of his Christ, and he will reign forever and ever (Revelation 11:15).

The Zionism of Man asked, "Lord, are you at this time going to restore the kingdom to Israel?" and the Zionism of God replied, "It is not for you to know the times or dates the Father has set by his own authority" (Acts 1:6-7).

The Zionism of God sovereignly raised Israel from the ashes, resurrected a dead language, preserved a remnant of Jewish believers and will one day fulfill every prophecy concerning Zion. The Zionism of Man buys tanks for secular Israel, applauds its campaign of ethnic cleansing, encourages it to forcibly restore its ancient boundaries and ignores its sins.

The tension between the Zionism of man and God began when Ishmael was conceived and continues to this day. But its struggles are not a war between the descendants of Ishmael and Isaac or Arab and Jew. They are an echo of an even more devastating war – the war between faith and presumption – two unequal and opposite polls in the realms of Heaven.

The fruit of God's Zionism is love, joy, peace, patience, kindness, goodness, faithfulness, gentleness and self-control

The fruit of Man's Zionism is hatred, despair, hostility, intolerance, malice, iniquity, treachery, brutality and unrestraint.

Only God's Zionism will prevail – because love never fails.

Appendix III

The Declaration Of The Establishment Of The State Of Israel

On May 14, 1948, on the day in which the British Mandate over a Palestine expired, the Jewish People's Council gathered at the Tel Aviv Museum, and approved the following proclamation, declaring the establishment of the State of Israel. The new state was recognized that night at 11:00 AM Israel time by the United States and three days later by the USSR.

ERETZ ISRAEL (the Land of Israel) was the birthplace of the Jewish people. Here their spiritual, religious and political identity was shaped. Here they first attained to statehood, created cultural values of national and universal significance and gave to the world the eternal Book of Books.

After being forcibly exiled from their land, the people kept faith with it throughout their Dispersion and never ceased to pray and hope for their return to it and for the restoration in it of their political freedom.

Impelled by this historic and traditional attachment, Jews strove in every successive generation to reestablish themselves in their ancient homeland. In recent decades they returned in their masses. Pioneers, ma'pilim (immigrants coming to Eretz Israel in defiance of restrictive legislation) and defenders, they made deserts bloom, revived the Hebrew language, built villages and towns, and created a thriving community controlling its own economy and culture, loving peace but knowing how to defend itself, bringing the blessings of progress to all the country's inhabitants, and aspiring towards independent nationhood.

In the year 5657 (1897), at the summons of the spiritual father of the Jewish State, Theodore Herzl, the First Zionist Congress convened and proclaimed the right of the Jewish people to national rebirth in its own country.

This right was recognized in the Balfour Declaration of the 2nd November, 1917, and reaffirmed in the Mandate of the League of Nations which, in particular, gave international sanction to the historic connection between the Jewish people and Eretz Israel and to the right of the Jewish people to rebuild its National Home.

The catastrophe which recently befell the Jewish people the massacre of millions of Jews in Europe was another clear demonstration of the urgency of solving the problem of its homelessness by reestablishing in Eretz Israel the Jewish State, which would open the gates of the homeland wide to every Jew and confer upon the Jewish people the status of a fully privileged member of the community of nations.

Survivors of the Nazi holocaust in Europe, as well as Jews from other parts of the world, continued to migrate to Eretz Israel, undaunted by difficulties, restrictions and dangers, and never ceased to assert their right to a life of dignity, freedom and honest toil in their national homeland.

In the Second World War, the Jewish community of this country contributed its full share to the struggle of the freedom and peace-loving nations against the forces of Nazi wickedness and, by the blood of its soldiers and its war effort, gained the right to be reckoned among the peoples who founded the United Nations.

On the 29th November, 1947, the United Nations General Assembly passed a resolution calling for the establishment of a Jewish State in Eretz Israel; the General Assembly required the inhabitants of Eretz Israel to take such steps as were necessary on their part for the implementation of that resolution. This recognition by the United Nations of the right of the Jewish people to establish their State is irrevocable.

This right is the natural right of the Jewish people to be masters of their own fate, like all other nations, in their own sovereign State.

ACCORDINGLY WE, MEMBERS OF THE PEOPLE'S COUNCIL, REPRESENTATIVES OF THE JEWISH COMMUNITY OF ERETZ-ISRAEL AND OF THE ZIONIST MOVEMENT, ARE HERE ASSEMBLED ON THE DAY OF THE TERMINATION OF THE BRITISH MANDATE OVER ERETZISRAEL AND, BY VIRTUE OF OUR NATURAL AND HISTORIC RIGHT AND ON THE STRENGTH OF THE RESOLUTION OF THE UNITED NATIONS GENERAL ASSEMBLY, HEREBY DECLARE THE ESTABLISHMENT OF A JEWISH STATE IN ERETZISRAEL, TO BE KNOWN AS THE STATE OF ISRAEL.

WE DECLARE that, with effect from the moment of the termination of the Mandate being tonight, the eve of Sabbath, the 6th Iyar, 5708 (15th May, 1948), until the establishment of the elected, regular authorities of the State in accordance with the Constitution which shall be adopted by the Elected Constituent Assembly not later than the 1st October 1948, the People's Council shall act as a Provisional Council of State, and its executive organ, the People's Administration, shall be the Provisional Government of the Jewish State, to be called "Israel".

THE STATE OF ISRAEL will be open for Jewish immigration and for the Ingathering of the Exiles; it will foster the development of the country for the benefit of all its inhabitants; it will be based on freedom, justice and peace as envisaged by the prophets of Israel; it will ensure complete equality of social and political rights to all its inhabitants irrespective of religion, race or sex; it will guarantee freedom of religion, conscience, language, education and culture; it will safeguard the Holy Places of all religions; and it will be faithful to the principles of the Charter of the United Nations.

THE STATE OF ISRAEL is prepared to cooperate with the agencies and representatives of the United Nations in implementing the resolution of the General Assembly of the 29th November, 1947, and will take steps to bring about the economic union of the whole of Eretz Israel.

WE APPEAL to the United Nations to assist the Jewish people

in the building up of its State and to receive the State of Israel into the comity of nations.

WE APPEAL in the very midst of the onslaught launched against us now for months to the Arab inhabitants of the State of Israel to preserve peace and participate in the upbuilding of the State on the basis of full and equal citizenship and due representation in all its provisional and permanent institutions.

WE EXTEND our hand to all neighboring states and their peoples in an offer of peace and good neighborliness, and appeal to them to establish bonds of cooperation and mutual help with the sovereign Jewish people settled in its own land. The State of Israel is prepared to do its share in a common effort for the advancement of the entire Middle East.

WE APPEAL to the Jewish people throughout the Diaspora to rally round the Jews of Eretz Israel in the tasks of immigration and upbuilding and to stand by them in the great struggle for the realization of the age-old dream the redemption of Israel.

PLACING OUR TRUST IN THE ALMIGHTY, WE AFFIX OUR SIGNATURES TO THIS PROCLAMATION AT THIS SESSION OF THE PROVISIONAL COUNCIL OF STATE, ON THE SOIL OF THE HOMELAND, IN THE CITY OF TELAVIV, ON THIS SABBATH EVE, THE 5TH DAY OF IYAR, 5708 (14TH MAY,1948).

David BenGurion
Rabbi Kalman Kahana
Aharon Zisling
Yitzchak Ben Zvi
Saadia Kobashi
Daniel Auster
Rachel Cohen
David Zvi Pinkas
Mordekhai Bentov
Moshe Kolodny
Eliyahu Berligne
Rabbi Yitzchak Meir Levin
Eliezer Kaplan

Fritz Bernstein
Abraham Katznelson
Rabbi Wolf Gold
Meir David Loewenstein
Felix Rosenblueth
Meir Grabovsky
David Remez
Yitzchak Gruenbaum
Zvi Luria
Berl Repetur
Dr. Abraham Granovsky
Golda Myerson
Mordekhai Shattner
Nachum Nir
Ben Zion Sternberg
Eliyahu Dobkin
Zvi Segal
Bekhor Shitreet
Meir WilnerKovner
Rabbi Yehuda Leib Hacohen Fishman
Moshe Shapira
Zerach Wahrhaftig
Moshe Shertok
Herzl Vardi

Appendix IV

United Nations Security Council Resolution 242

22 November 1967

The Security Council,

Expressing its continuing concern with the grave situation in the Middle East,

Emphasizing the inadmissibility of the acquisition of territory by war and the need to work for a just and lasting peace, in which every State in the area can live in security,

Emphasizing further that all Member States in their acceptance of the Charter of the United Nations have undertaken a commitment to act in accordance with Article 2 of the Charter,

1. *Affirms* that the fulfillment of Charter principles requires the establishment of a just and lasting peace in the Middle East which should include the application of both the following principles:

(i) Withdrawal of Israel armed forces from territories occupied in the recent conflict;

(ii) Termination of all claims or states of belligerency and respect for and acknowledgement of the sovereignty, territorial integrity and political independence of every State in the area and their right to live in peace within secure and recognized boundaries free from threats or acts of force:

2. *Affirms further* the necessity

(a) For guaranteeing freedom of navigation through international waterways in the area;

(b) For achieving a just settlement of the refugee problem;

(c) For guaranteeing the territorial inviolability and political independence of every State in the area, through measures including the establishment of demilitarized zones;

3. *Requests* the Secretary-General to designate a Special Representative to proceed to the Middle East to establish and maintain contacts with the States concerned in order to promote agreement and assist efforts to achieve a peaceful and accepted settlement in accordance with the provisions and principles in this resolution;

4. *Requests* the Secretary-General to report to the Security Council on the progress of the efforts of the Special Representative as soon as possible.

Adopted unanimously at the 1382nd meeting.

Appendix V

United Nations Security Council Resolution 338

22 October 1973

The Security Council,

1. *Calls upon* all parties to the present fighting to cease all firing and terminate all military activity immediately, no later than 12 hours after the moment of the adoption of this decision, in the positions they now occupy;

2. *Calls upon* the parties concerned to start immediately after the cease-fire the implementation of Security Council resolution 242 (1967) in all of its parts;

3. *Decides* that, immediately and concurrently with the cease-fire, negotiations shall start between the parties concerned under appropriate auspices aimed at establishing a just and durable peace in the Middle East.

Adopted at the 1747th meeting by 14 votes to none[27]

[27] One member (China) did not participate in the voting.

Appendix VI

The Camp David Accords

The Framework for Peace in the Middle East

Muhammad Anwar al-Sadat, President of the Arab Republic of Egypt, and Menachem Begin, Prime Minister of Israel, met with Jimmy Carter, President of the United States of America, at Camp David from September 5 to September 17, 1978, and have agreed on the following framework for peace in the Middle East. They invite other parties to the Arab-Israel conflict to adhere to it.

Preamble

The search for peace in the Middle East must be guided by the following:

The agreed basis for a peaceful settlement of the conflict between Israel and its neighbors is United Nations Security Council Resolution 242, in all its parts.

After four wars during 30 years, despite intensive human efforts, the Middle East, which is the cradle of civilization and the birthplace of three great religions, does not enjoy the blessings of peace. The people of the Middle East yearn for peace so that the vast human and natural resources of the region can be turned to the pursuits of peace and so that this area can become a model for coexistence and cooperation among nations.

The historic initiative of President Sadat in visiting Jerusalem and the reception accorded to him by the parliament, government and people of Israel, and the reciprocal visit of Prime Minister Begin to Ismailia, the peace proposals made by both leaders, as well as the warm reception of these missions by the peoples of both countries, have created an unprecedented opportunity for peace which must not be lost if this generation and future generations are to be spared the tragedies of war.

The provisions of the Charter of the United Nations and the other accepted norms of international law and legitimacy now provide accepted standards for the conduct of relations among all states.

To achieve a relationship of peace, in the spirit of Article 2 of the United Nations Charter, future negotiations between Israel and any neighbor prepared to negotiate peace and security with it are necessary for the purpose of carrying out all the provisions and principles of Resolutions 242 and 338.

Peace requires respect for the sovereignty, territorial integrity and political independence of every state in the area and their right to live in peace within secure and recognized boundaries free from threats or acts of force. Progress toward that goal can accelerate movement toward a new era of reconciliation in the Middle East marked by cooperation in promoting economic development, in maintaining stability and in assuring security.

Security is enhanced by a relationship of peace and by cooperation between nations which enjoy normal relations. In addition, under the terms of peace treaties, the parties can, on the basis of reciprocity, agree to special security arrangements such as demilitarized zones, limited armaments areas, early warning stations, the presence of international forces, liaison, agreed measures for monitoring and other arrangements that they agree are useful.

Framework

Taking these factors into account, the parties are determined to reach a just, comprehensive, and durable settlement of the Middle East conflict through the conclusion of peace treaties based on Security Council resolutions 242 and 338 in all their parts. Their purpose is to achieve peace and good neighborly relations. They recognize that for peace to endure, it must involve all those who have been most deeply affected by the conflict. They therefore agree that this framework, as appropriate, is intended by them to constitute a basis for peace not only between Egypt and Israel, but also between Israel and each of its other neighbors which is prepared to negotiate peace with Israel on this basis. With that objective in mind, they have agreed to proceed as follows:

West Bank and Gaza

Egypt, Israel, Jordan and the representatives of the Palestinian people should participate in negotiations on the resolution of the Palestinian problem in all its aspects. To achieve that objective, negotiations relating to the West Bank and Gaza should proceed in three stages:

Egypt and Israel agree that, in order to ensure a peaceful and orderly transfer of authority, and taking into account the security concerns of all the parties, there should be transitional arrangements for the West Bank and Gaza for a period not exceeding five years. In order to provide full autonomy to the inhabitants, under these arrangements the Israeli military government and its civilian administration will be withdrawn as soon as a self-governing authority has been freely elected by the inhabitants of these areas to replace the existing military government. To negotiate the details of a transitional arrangement, Jordan will be invited to join the negotiations on the basis of this framework. These new arrangements should give due consideration both to the principle of self-government by the inhabitants of these territories and to the legitimate security concerns of the parties involved.

Egypt, Israel, and Jordan will agree on the modalities for establishing elected self-governing authority in the West Bank and Gaza. The delegations of Egypt and Jordan may include Palestinians from the West Bank and Gaza or other Palestinians as mutually agreed. The parties will negotiate an agreement which will define the powers and responsibilities of the self-governing authority to be exercised in the West Bank and Gaza. A withdrawal of Israeli armed forces will take place and there will be a redeployment of the remaining Israeli forces into specified security locations. The agreement will also include arrangements for assuring internal and external security and public order. A strong local police force will be established, which may include Jordanian citizens. In addition, Israeli and Jordanian forces will participate in joint patrols and in the manning of control posts to assure the security of the borders.

When the self-governing authority (administrative council) in the West Bank and Gaza is established and inaugurated, the transitional period of five years will begin. As soon as possible, but not later than the third year after the beginning of the transitional period, negotiations will take place to determine the final status of the West Bank and Gaza and its relationship with its neighbors and to conclude a peace treaty between Israel and Jordan by the end of the transitional period. These negotiations will be conducted among Egypt, Israel, Jordan and the elected representatives of the inhabitants of the West Bank and Gaza. Two separate but related committees will be convened, one committee, consisting of representatives of the four parties which will negotiate and agree on the final status of the West Bank and Gaza, and its relationship with its neighbors, and the second committee, consisting of representatives of Israel and representatives of Jordan to be joined by the elected representatives of the inhabitants of the West Bank and Gaza, to negotiate the peace treaty between Israel and Jordan, taking into account the agreement reached in the final status of the West Bank and Gaza. The negotiations shall be based on all the provisions and principles of UN Security Council Resolution 242. The negotiations will resolve, among other matters, the location of the boundaries and the nature of the security arrangements. The solution from the negotiations must also recognize the legitimate right of the Palestinian peoples and their just requirements. In this way, the Palestinians will participate in the determination of their own future through:

The negotiations among Egypt, Israel, Jordan and the representatives of the inhabitants of the West Bank and Gaza to agree on the final status of the West Bank and Gaza and other outstanding issues by the end of the transitional period.

Submitting their agreements to a vote by the elected representatives of the inhabitants of the West Bank and Gaza.

Providing for the elected representatives of the inhabitants of the West Bank and Gaza to decide how they shall govern themselves consistent with the provisions of their agreement.

Participating as stated above in the work of the committee negotiating the peace treaty between Israel and Jordan.

All necessary measures will be taken and provisions made to assure the security of Israel and its neighbors during the transitional period and beyond. To assist in providing such security, a strong local police force will be constituted by the self-governing authority. It will be composed of inhabitants of the West Bank and Gaza. The police will maintain liaison on internal security matters with the designated Israeli, Jordanian, and Egyptian officers.

During the transitional period, representatives of Egypt, Israel, Jordan, and the self-governing authority will constitute a continuing committee to decide by agreement on the modalities of admission of persons displaced from the West Bank and Gaza in 1967, together with necessary measures to prevent disruption and disorder. Other matters of common concern may also be dealt with by this committee.

Egypt and Israel will work with each other and with other interested parties to establish agreed procedures for a prompt, just and permanent implementation of the resolution of the refugee problem.

Egypt-Israel

Egypt-Israel undertake not to resort to the threat or the use of force to settle disputes. Any disputes shall be settled by peaceful means in accordance with the provisions of Article 33 of the U.N. Charter.

In order to achieve peace between them, the parties agree to negotiate in good faith with a goal of concluding within three months from the signing of the Framework a peace treaty between them while inviting the other parties to the conflict to proceed simultaneously to negotiate and conclude similar peace treaties with a view the achieving a comprehensive peace in the area. The Framework for the Conclusion of a Peace Treaty between Egypt and Israel will govern the peace negotiations between them. The parties will agree on the modalities and the timetable for the implementation of their obligations under the treaty.

Associated Principles

Egypt and Israel state that the principles and provisions described below should apply to peace treaties between Israel and each of its neighbors — Egypt, Jordan, Syria and Lebanon.

Signatories shall establish among themselves relationships normal to states at peace with one another. To this end, they should undertake to abide by all the provisions of the U.N. Charter. Steps to be taken in this respect include:

full recognition;

abolishing economic boycotts;

guaranteeing that under their jurisdiction the citizens of the other parties shall enjoy the protection of the due process of law.

Signatories should explore possibilities for economic development in the context of final peace treaties, with the objective of contributing to the atmosphere of peace, cooperation and friendship which is their common goal.

Claims commissions may be established for the mutual settlement of all financial claims.

The United States shall be invited to participated in the talks on matters related to the modalities of the implementation of the agreements and working out the timetable for the carrying out of the obligations of the parties.

The United Nations Security Council shall be requested to endorse the peace treaties and ensure that their provisions shall not be violated. The permanent members of the Security Council shall be requested to underwrite the peace treaties and ensure respect or the provisions. They shall be requested to conform their policies an actions with the undertaking contained in this Framework.

For the Government of Israel:
Menachem Begin

For the Government of
the Arab Republic of Egypt
Muhammad Anwar al-Sadat

Witnessed by
Jimmy Carter,
President of the United States of America

Framework for the Conclusion of a Peace Treaty between Egypt and Israel

In order to achieve peace between them, Israel and Egypt agree to negotiate in good faith with a goal of concluding within three months of the signing of this framework a peace treaty between them:

It is agreed that:

The site of the negotiations will be under a United Nations flag at a location or locations to be mutually agreed.

All of the principles of U.N. Resolution 242 will apply in this resolution of the dispute between Israel and Egypt.

Unless otherwise mutually agreed, terms of the peace treaty will be implemented between two and three years after the peace treaty is signed.

The following matters are agreed between the parties:

the full exercise of Egyptian sovereignty up to the internationally recognized border between Egypt and mandated Palestine;

the withdrawal of Israeli armed forces from the Sinai;

the use of airfields left by the Israelis near al-Arish, Rafah, Ras en-Naqb, and Sharm el-Sheikh for civilian purposes only, including possible commercial use only by all nations;

the right of free passage by ships of Israel through the Gulf of Suez and the Suez Canal on the basis of the Constantinople Convention of 1888 applying to all nations; the Strait of Tiran and Gulf of Aqaba are international waterways to be open to all nations for unimpeded and nonsuspendable freedom of navigation and overflight;

the construction of a highway between the Sinai and Jordan near Eilat with guaranteed free and peaceful passage by Egypt and Jordan; and

the stationing of military forces listed below.

Stationing of Forces

No more than one division (mechanized or infantry) of Egyptian armed forces will be stationed within an area lying approximately 50 km. (30 miles) east of the Gulf of Suez and the Suez Canal.

Only United Nations forces and civil police equipped with light weapons to perform normal police functions will be stationed within an area lying west of the international border and the Gulf of Aqaba, varying in width from 20 km. (12 miles) to 40 km. (24 miles).

In the area within 3 km. (1.8 miles) east of the international border there will be Israeli limited military forces not to exceed four infantry battalions and United Nations observers.

Border patrol units not to exceed three battalions will supplement the civil police in maintaining order in the area not included above.

The exact demarcation of the above areas will be as decided during the peace negotiations.

Early warning stations may exist to insure compliance with the terms of the agreement.

United Nations forces will be stationed:

in part of the area in the Sinai lying within about 20 km. of the Mediterranean Sea and adjacent to the international border, and

in the Sharm el-Sheikh area to insure freedom of passage through the Strait of Tiran; and these forces will not be removed unless such removal is approved by the Security Council of the United Nations with a unanimous vote of the five permanent members.

After a peace treaty is signed, and after the interim withdrawal is complete, normal relations will be established between Egypt and Israel, including full recognition, including diplomatic, economic and cultural relations; termination of economic boycotts and barriers to the free movement of goods and people; and mutual protection of citizens by the due process of law.

Interim Withdrawal

Between three months and nine months after the signing of the peace treaty, all Israeli forces will withdraw east of a line extending from a point east of El-Arish to Ras Muhammad, the exact location of this line to be determined by mutual agreement.

For the Government of
the Arab Republic of Egypt:
Muhammad Anwar al-Sadat

For the Government of Israel:
Menachem Begin

Witnessed by:
Jimmy Carter,
President of the United States of America

Source: U.S. Department of State's Office of International Information Programs

Appendix VII

Excerpts from the Oslo II Peace Accords, known officially as:

Israeli-Palestinian Interim Agreement on the West Bank and the Gaza Strip

Washington, D.C., September 28, 1995

(Signed by Israeli Prime Minister Yitzhak Rabin and PLO Chairman Yasir Arafat and witnessed by U.S. President Bill Clinton, Egyptian President Hosni Mubarak, King Hussein of Jordan and the leaders of The Russian Federation, the Kingdom of Norway and The European Union.)

The Government of the State of Israel and the Palestine Liberation Organization (hereinafter "the PLO"), the representative of the Palestinian people;

PREAMBLE

WITHIN the framework of the Middle East peace process initiated at Madrid in October 1991;

REAFFIRMING their determination to put an end to decades of confrontation and to live in peaceful coexistence, mutual dignity and security, while recognizing their mutual legitimate and political rights;

REAFFIRMING their desire to achieve a just, lasting and comprehensive peace settlement and historic reconciliation through the agreed political process;

RECOGNIZING that the peace process and the new era that it has created, as well as the new relationship established between the two Parties as described above, are irreversible, and the determination of the two Parties to maintain, sustain and continue the peace process;

RECOGNIZING that the aim of the Israeli-Palestinian negotiations within the current Middle East peace process is, among other things, to establish a Palestinian Interim Self-Government Authority, i.e. the elected Council (hereinafter "the Council" or "the Palestinian Council"), and the elected Ra'ees of the Executive Authority, for the Palestinian people in the West Bank and the Gaza Strip, for a transitional period not exceeding five years from the date of signing the Agreement on the Gaza Strip and the Jericho Area (hereinafter "the Gaza-Jericho Agreement") on May 4, 1994, leading to a permanent settlement based on Security Council Resolutions 242 and 338;

REAFFIRMING their understanding that the interim self-government arrangements contained in this Agreement are an integral part of the whole peace process, that the negotiations on the permanent status, that will start as soon as possible but not later than May 4, 1996, will lead to the implementation of Security Council Resolutions 242 and 338, and that the Interim Agreement shall settle all the issues of the interim period and that no such issues will be deferred to the agenda of the permanent status negotiations;

REAFFIRMING their adherence to the mutual recognition and commitments expressed in the letters dated September 9, 1993, signed by and exchanged between the Prime Minister of Israel and the Chairman of the PLO;

DESIROUS of putting into effect the signed at Washington, D.C. on September 13, 1993, and the Agreed Minutes thereto (hereinafter "the DOP") and in particular Article III and Annex I concerning the holding of direct, free and general political elections for the Council and the Ra'ees of the Executive Authority in order that the Palestinian people in the West Bank, Jerusalem and the Gaza Strip may democratically elect accountable representatives;

RECOGNIZING that these elections will constitute a significant interim preparatory step toward the realization of the legitimate rights of the Palestinian people and their just requirements and will provide a democratic basis for the establishment of Palestinian institutions;

REAFFIRMING their mutual commitment to act, in accordance with this Agreement, immediately, efficiently and effectively against acts or threats of terrorism, violence or incitement, whether committed by Palestinians or Israelis;

FOLLOWING the <u>GAZA-JERICHO AGREEMENT;</u> the signed at Erez on August 29, 1994 (hereinafter "the Preparatory Transfer Agreement"); and the Protocol on Further Transfer of Powers and Responsibilities signed at Cairo on August 27, 1995 (hereinafter "the Further Transfer Protocol"); which three agreements will be superseded by this Agreement;

HEREBY AGREE as follows:

CHAPTER I - THE COUNCIL

ARTICLE I

Transfer of Authority

1. Israel shall transfer powers and responsibilities as specified in this Agreement from the Israeli military government and its Civil Administration to the Council in accordance with this Agreement. Israel shall continue to exercise powers and responsibilities not so transferred.

*   *   *   *

CHAPTER II - REDEPLOYMENT AND SECURITY ARRANGEMENTS

ARTICLE X

Redeployment of Isreali Military Forces

1. The first phase of the Israeli military forces redeployment will cover populated areas in the West Bank - cities, towns, villages, refugee camps and hamlets - as set out in <u>ANNEX I</u>, and will be completed prior to the eve of the Palestinian elections, i. e., 22 days before the day of the elections.

2. Further redeployments of Israeli military forces to specified military locations will commence after the inauguration of the Council and will be gradually implemented commensurate with the assumption of responsibility for public order and internal security by the Palestinian Police, to be completed within 18 months from the date of the inauguration of the Council as detailed in <u>ARTICLES XI (LAND)</u> and <u>XIII (SECURITY)</u>, below and in <u>ANNEX I</u>.

3. The Palestinian Police shall be deployed and shall assume responsibility for public order and internal security for Palestinians in a phased manner in accordance with <u>XIII (SECURITY)</u> below and <u>ANNEX I</u>.

4. Israel shall continue to carry the responsibility for external security, as well as the responsibility for overall security of Israelis for the purpose of safeguarding their internal security and public order.

5. For the purpose of this Agreement, "Israeli military forces" includes Israel Police and other Israeli security forces.

*   *   *   *

ARTICLE XI
Land

1. The two sides view the West Bank and the Gaza Strip as a single territorial unit, the integrity and status of which will be preserved during the interim period.

2. The two sides agree that West Bank and Gaza Strip territory, except for issues that will be negotiated in the permanent status negotiations, will come under the jurisdiction of the Palestinian

Council in a phased manner, to be completed within 18 months from the date of the inauguration of the Council, as specified below:

a. Land in populated areas (Areas A and B), including government and Al Waqf land, will come under the jurisdiction of the Council during the first phase of redeployment.

b. All civil powers and responsibilities, including planning and zoning, in Areas A and B, set out in ANNEX III, will be transferred to and assumed by the Council during the first phase of redeployment.

c. In Area C, during the first phase of redeployment Israel will transfer to the Council civil powers and responsibilities not relating to territory, as set out in ANNEX III.

d. The further redeployments of Israeli military forces to specified military locations will be gradually implemented in accordance with the DOP in three phases, each to take place after an interval of six months, after the inauguration of the Council, to be completed within 18 months from the date of the inauguration of the Council.

e. During the further redeployment phases to be completed within 18 months from the date of the inauguration of the Council, powers and responsibilities relating to territory will be transferred gradually to Palestinian jurisdiction that will cover West Bank and Gaza Strip territory, except for the issues that will be negotiated in the permanent status negotiations.

f. The specified military locations referred to in Article X, paragraph 2 above will be determined in the further redeployment phases, within the specified time-frame ending not later than 18 months from the date of the inauguration of the Council, and will be negotiated in the permanent status negotiations.

3. For the purpose of this Agreement and until the completion of the first phase of the further redeployments:

a. "Area A" means the populated areas delineated by a red line and shaded in brown on attached MAP NO. 1;

b. "Area B" means the populated areas delineated by a red line and shaded in yellow on attached MAP NO. 1, and the built-up area of the hamlets listed in APPENDIX 6 TO ANNEX I, and

c. "Area C" means areas of the West Bank outside Areas A and B, which, except for the issues that will be negotiated in the permanent status negotiations, will be gradually transferred to Palestinian jurisdiction in accordance with this Agreement.

*   *   *   *

ARTICLE XII

Arrangements for Security and Public Order

1. In order to guarantee public order and internal security for the Palestinians of the West Bank and the Gaza Strip, the Council shall establish a strong police force as set out in Article XIV below. Israel shall continue to carry the responsibility for defense against external threats, including the responsibility for protecting the Egyptian and Jordanian borders, and for defense against external threats from the sea and from the air, as well as the responsibility for overall security of Israelis and Settlements, for the purpose of safeguarding their internal security and public order, and will have all the powers to take the steps necessary to meet this responsibility.

*   *   *   *

ARTICLE XIV

The Palestinian Police

1. The Council shall establish a strong police force. The duties, functions, structure, deployment and composition of the Palestinian Police, together with provisions regarding its equipment and operation, as well as rules of conduct, are set out in ANNEX I.

2. The Palestinian police force established under the Gaza-Jericho Agreement will be fully integrated into the Palestinian Police and will be subject to the provisions of this Agreement.

3. Except for the Palestinian Police and the Israeli military forces, no other armed forces shall be established or operate in the West Bank and the Gaza Strip.

4. Except for the arms, ammunition and equipment of the Palestinian Police described in ANNEX I, and those of the Israeli military forces, no organization, group or individual in the West Bank and the Gaza Strip shall manufacture, sell, acquire, possess, import or otherwise introduce into the West Bank or the Gaza Strip any firearms, ammunition, weapons, explosives, gunpowder or any related equipment, unless otherwise provided for in Annex I.

ARTICLE XV

Prevention of Hostile Acts

1. Both sides shall take all measures necessary in order to prevent acts of terrorism, crime and hostilities directed against each other, against individuals falling under the other's authority and against their property and shall take legal measures against offenders.

*   *   *   *

ARTICLE XVI

Confidence Building Measures

With a view to fostering a positive and supportive public atmosphere to accompany the implementation of this Agreement, to establish a solid basis of mutual trust and good faith, and in order to facilitate the anticipated cooperation and new relations between the two peoples, both Parties agree to carry out confidence building measures as detailed herewith:

1. Israel will release or turn over to the Palestinian side, Palestinian detainees and prisoners, residents of the West Bank and the Gaza Strip. The first stage of release of these prisoners and detainees will take place on the signing of this Agreement and the second stage will take place prior to the date of the elections. There will be a third stage of release of detainees and prisoners. Detainees and prisoners will be released from among categories detailed in ANNEX VII (Release of Palestinian Prisoners and Detainees). Those released will be free to return to their homes in the West Bank and the Gaza Strip.

2. Palestinians who have maintained contact with the Israeli authorities will not be subjected to acts of harassment, violence, retribution or prosecution. Appropriate ongoing measures will be taken, in coordination with Israel, in order to ensure their protection.

3. Palestinians from abroad whose entry into the West Bank and the Gaza Strip is approved pursuant to this Agreement, and to whom the provisions of this Article are applicable, will not be prosecuted for offenses committed prior to September 13, 1993.

*   *   *   *

Human Rights and the Rule of Law

Israel and the Council shall exercise their powers and responsibilities pursuant to this Agreement with due regard to internationally-accepted norms and principles of human rights and the rule of law.

*   *   *   *

CHAPTER 5 - MISCELLANEOUS PROVISIONS

ARTICLE XXIX
Safe Passage between the West Bank and the Gaza Strip

Arrangements for safe passage of persons and transportation between the West Bank and the Gaza Strip are set out in <u>ANNEX I</u>.

*   *   *   *

ARTICLE XXXI

Final Clauses

1. This Agreement shall enter into force on the date of its signing.

2. The Gaza-Jericho Agreement, except for Article XX (Confidence-Building Measures), the Preparatory Transfer Agreement and the Further Transfer Protocol will be superseded by this Agreement.

3. The Council, upon its inauguration, shall replace the Palestinian Authority and shall assume all the undertakings and obligations of the Palestinian Authority under the Gaza-Jericho Agreement, the Preparatory Transfer Agreement, and the Further Transfer Protocol.

4. The two sides shall pass all necessary legislation to implement this Agreement.

5. Permanent status negotiations will commence as soon as possible, but not later than May 4, 1996, between the Parties. It is understood that these negotiations shall cover remaining issues, including: Jerusalem, refugees, settlements, security arrangements, borders, relations and cooperation with other neighbors, and other issues of common interest.

6. Nothing in this Agreement shall prejudice or preempt the outcome of the negotiations on the permanent status to be conducted pursuant to the DOP. Neither Party shall be deemed, by virtue of having entered into this Agreement, to have renounced or waived any of its existing rights, claims or positions.

7. Neither side shall initiate or take any step that will change the status of the West Bank and the Gaza Strip pending the outcome of the permanent status negotiations.

8. The two Parties view the West Bank and the Gaza Strip as a single territorial unit, the integrity and status of which will be preserved during the interim period.

9. The PLO undertakes that, within two months of the date of the inauguration of the Council, the Palestinian National Council will convene and formally approve the necessary changes in regard to the Palestinian Covenant, as undertaken in the letters signed by the Chairman of the PLO and addressed to the Prime Minister of Israel, dated September 9, 1993 and May 4, 1994.

10. Pursuant to ANNEX I, ARTICLE IX of this Agreement, Israel confirms that the permanent checkpoints on the roads leading to and from the Jericho Area (except those related to the access road leading from Mousa Alami to the Allenby Bridge) will be removed upon the completion of the first phase of redeployment.

11. Prisoners who, pursuant to the Gaza-Jericho Agreement, were turned over to the Palestinian Authority on the condition that they remain in the Jericho Area for the remainder of their sentence, will be free to return to their homes in the West Bank and the Gaza Strip upon the completion of the first phase of redeployment.

Done at Washington DC, this 28th day of September, 1995.

Author's Profile

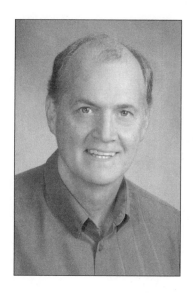

JACK KINCAID has worked in television management and production for over 20 years. He has coordinated and funded Christian television projects and humanitarian efforts throughout the world. Currently he is the President and CEO of Banner communications, Inc., a non-profit missionary media organization.

He is the father of three children and resides in Florida with his wife, Lisa and daughter Kennedy Joy.